Stephen Alfred Forbes

Insect injuries to the seed and root of Indian corn

Stephen Alfred Forbes

Insect injuries to the seed and root of Indian corn

ISBN/EAN: 9783337303891

Printed in Europe, USA, Canada, Australia, Japan

Cover: Foto ©ninafisch / pixelio.de

More available books at **www.hansebooks.com**

UNIVERSITY OF ILLINOIS,

Agricultural Experiment Station.

URBANA, MAY, 1896.

BULLETIN NO. 44.

INSECT INJURIES TO THE SEED AND ROOT OF INDIAN CORN.*

INTRODUCTORY.

The corn insects now recognized as in some way and to some extent injurious to some part of the plant number 214 species, of which 18 are known to infest the seed, 27 the root and the subterranean part of the stalk, 76 the stalk above ground, 118 the leaf, 19 the blossom,—that is the tassel and the silk,—42 the ear in the field, 2 the stacked fodder, and 24 the corn in store, either whole or ground. The greater part of this long list, which is doubtless by no means really complete, is composed of those whose injuries are now so slight or rare as to constitute a possible menace rather than to cause a serious loss; but the history of economic entomology, and even of the entomology of this one plant, teaches us that we can rarely tell in advance what to expect of any possibly injurious species. In fact, some of the insect enemies of corn now most destructive were not many years ago almost unknown even to the entomologist—the northern corn root worm and the corn root aphis, for example.

The principal insect species infesting this plant are the seed-corn maggot and the wireworms, attacking the seed; these latter

---

*This article is an abstract, with occasional minor alterations, of the more strictly economic parts of the Seventh Report of the writer as State Entomologist of Illinois, first published in February, 1895.

insects, the white grubs, the corn root worms, and the root aphis, affecting the roots; the cutworms and root web-worms, the army worm, the stalk-borer, the corn worm, the bill-bugs, the chinch bug, the corn flea-beetle, and the grasshoppers, injuring stalk and leaf; the corn worm, the corn root worms, and the grasshoppers, eating the flower structures and the ear; and the meal-moth and the weevils devouring the kernel in the granary or the meal in the bin. Of these, by far the worst at present are the wireworms, the corn root worms, the white grubs, the root lice, the cutworms, the chinch bug, the grasshoppers, and the army worm.

The most serious ordinary injuries to corn, those which the plant is least able to sustain, are injurious to the seed and root, particularly those occurring early in the year; but they are, fortunately, those against which precautionary or preventive measures may be most readily taken, and with the best effect.

GENERAL INDICATIONS OF INJURY.

Before beginning a description of injuries to each part of the plant, a few practical hints may be given which will aid to a recognition of insect attack from the general aspect of the field or from the appearance of the entire plant.

1. If corn largely fails to appear in due time after planting, the farmer need not content himself with a surmise that his seed was poor or that the weather has been unfavorable, but should examine the seed itself for evidence of the work of one of several insects (*wireworms, seed-corn maggots, grass maggots, etc.*) attacking it in the earth.

2. If the young plants make an unequal start, some hills appearing earlier and growing more thriftily than others at the very first, the roots should be searched for the *corn root louse;* and even those hills should be examined in which the corn has not yet come up, as this louse sometimes infests the sprouting plant before it appears above ground.

3. The abundant occurrence of ants in the corn field, sinking their burrows among the stalks of the hill, is evidence of the presence of the *corn root louse* in their company.

4. If the growth of the corn is arrested or retarded in patches throughout the field, the leaves turning first yellow and then red, it is likely that the roots are infested by the same *root louse*, to be discovered by carefully digging up the hill and picking or gently shaking off the earth to expose the roots at their origin. If no insect enemy is found, the difficulty is quite likely to be due to a *fungus attack* known as the root blight of corn, a discussion of which does not come within the scope of this article. [See page 234.]

5. If single stalks or entire hills are killed or withered when a foot high or less, search should be made among the roots and on the stalk below the surface for the *wireworms* and the *white grubs.*

6. If the corn falls readily in a windy storm and does not afterward rise, and if it may be pulled up easily after the ear has begun to form, it is probable that the roots are infested by the *corn root worms* or that they have been eaten by *white grubs.*

7. If the plant remains green too long, maturing slowly, and if the field contains many sterile stalks or soft, imperfect nubbins, it is likely that the common *corn root worm*, in some of its stages, will be found in or among the roots if search be made before September 1. If large numbers of grass-green beetles one-fifth of an inch in length (about the size of a common red ladybug) are seen on the silks and tassels of the corn, or feeding upon the fallen pollen collected at the bases of the leaves, or upon the blossoms of ragweed or other flowering plants in the field, the crop has suffered from an attack of the *corn root worm*, of which these beetles are the adult, and the ground should be planted to some other crop the following year.

8. A deformed and unequal growth of the foliage, especially of that unfolding from the roll of leaves at the growing tip of the plant, with more or less irregular and ragged injury, when the corn is from one to two feet high, is often due to an attack by the first generation of the *corn worm*, the second generation of which burrows in the kernels of the ear of corn during late summer and early fall.

9. On the other hand, the presence of elongate holes, placed side by side in an orderly manner, in short rows extending across the well-opened leaf, is commonly the mark of an injury done when the corn was smaller by the *corn bill-bugs*, several species of which will be described when injuries to the leaf are under discussion.

10. An irregular eating away of the leaves of young corn, and a similarly irregular gnawing of the stalk near the ground when the plant is less than a foot in height, should lead to an examination of the earth about the base of the hill. If fine particles and small lumps of earth are found more or less closely webbed together in a mass approximating the size of a hickory nut, some one or more of the species of *root web-worms* are doubtless at work in the field.

11. The cutting of the young corn at or below the surface of the ground is an injury too well known as the work of the *cut-worms* to require more than bare mention here.

12. The appearance in the side of the stalk of a hole about the size of a straw, with a brown moist powder exuding, is evidence of

the presence of the *stalk-borer*, an insect which often does a great and practically irremediable damage to young corn in early spring, especially in low grounds, by burrowing the stalk, pushing more or less of its excrement out at the mouth of its burrow.

13.   A similar, equally evident burrowing of the ear, the excrement from which escapes by a hole through the green husks or becomes mixed through the silks at the tip of the ear, betrays the presence of the *corn worm* already mentioned under 8.

14.   The eating away of the blade of the leaf in late summer and autumn so as to make large irregular holes, which may multiply and increase in size until they finally leave only the stripped midrib and the bare stalk—the injury being commonly very much worse along the edges of the field—is commonly due to *grasshoppers*.

15.   In the corn crib or granary the commonest serious mischief is the peppering of the kernel with little round holes, each the diameter of the head of a pin, the first suspicion of which will frequently be aroused by the appearance of fine particles of meal sifting down somewhere within sight.   The insect most likely to be responsible for this mischief is the *corn moth;* but various *weevil species* may also be involved.

SYNOPSIS OF INJURIES.

A.   INJURIES TO THE SEED IN THE EARTH.

1.   Injuries by ants, which hollow out the kernel, commonly scattering the meal through the dirt.   Page 214 (Fig. 1 and 2.)

2.   Injuries by small beetles, which gnaw the kernel from without, commonly beginning at the germ.   Pages 215–217 (Fig. 3, 4, and 5.)

3.   Injuries by footless maggots, which bury themselves in the seed.   Page 218.

Seed-corn Maggot.   Page 218 (Fig. 6, 7, 8, and 9.)
Black-headed Grass Maggot.   Page 220 (Fig. 10.)

4.   Injuries by six-legged larvæ, which gnaw or bore through the kernel.   Page 220.

Pale-striped Flea-beetle.   Page 221 (Fig. 11, 12 and 13.)
The Banded Ips.   Page 222 (Fig. 14, 15, and 16.)
Wireworms.   Pages 224–233 (Fig. 17–32.)

B.   INJURIES TO THE ROOTS.

5.   Roots deadened, hardened, or dwarfed, without apparent loss of substance.   Page 235.

a. Small brown or yellowish ants abundant in the hills, and bluish green or whitish root lice (plant lice and mealy bugs) on the larger roots.   Page 235.

The Corn Root Aphis.   Page 237 (Fig. 33–37.)

The Grass Root Louse.   Pages 256, 257 (Fig. 40 and 41.)

b. No notable number of insects present.   The lowest roots dead; surface of underground part of stalk with brownish corroded spots, interior of this part darker, at least at the joints, while the spaces between may be seemingly healthy.   (Root blight of corn, a bacterial disease; not entomological.)   Page 234.

6.   Roots evidently injured or destroyed by perforations, gnawing, burrowing, decay or other loss of substance.   Page 257.

a. Roots eaten away, not burrowed or perforated, and without rotten or withered tips; tap-root commonly gone or decayed.   White grubs in soil among or beneath the roots.   Page 257.

White Grubs.   Pages 257–280 (Fig. 42–48.)

Prionus Grubs.   Page 281 (Fig. 49–51.)

b. Roots penetrated, perforated, irregularly burrowed, and more or less eaten off and eaten up.   Underground parts of stalk also similarly injured.   Page 282.

Wireworms in soil among the roots.   Pages 224–233 (Fig. 17–32.)

Small, slender, soft-bodied, yellowish white grubs in the roots and earth.   (The Southern Corn Root Worm.) Page 282 (Fig. 52–56.)

c. Roots visibly penetrated and perforated scarcely at all; sometimes decayed at tips, but not eaten away.   Principal injury interior, in form of minute burrows which are commonly longitudinal, discoverable on peeling or splitting the root, the burrows sometimes containing minute slender white six-legged larvæ, with brown head and neck and brown patch on last segment.   (The Northern Corn Root Worm.)   Page 287 (Fig. 57–61.)

DETAILED DISCUSSION OF INJURIES TO THE SEED.

*1. Injuries by ants, which hollow out the kernel, commonly scat-
tering the meal through the dirt.*

Injuries to corn by ants are of two kinds: one indirect but
serious; the other direct, but of little importance because quite
rare. The former will be treated in connection with insects affecting the root, since it is by rearing, transporting, and fostering
the root lice of corn that ants are most injurious; and the latter
is given here in its place as an injury to the seed in the earth.

Occasionally in searching for the causes of the failure of corn
to germinate, or to grow thriftily after making its appearance, a
kernel may be found wholly or partly hollowed out, the mealy
interior being not devoured, but scattered about in the earth,
while the outer shell of the seed remains but little disturbed. The
agents of this small mischief will frequently be found still buried
in the cavities they have excavated—most commonly ants of a
minute pale yellow species, a little more than a sixteenth of an
inch in length. This injury to corn requires no treatment so far
as is now known, and probably admits of none. I have seen two
species of ants engaged in this injury to planted corn in Illinois:
one the common little house ant*, which frequently becomes a
nuisance in pantries, especially if sugar is exposed to its visita-
tions (see Fig. 1); and the other a larger, outdoor species, well
shown in Fig. 2.

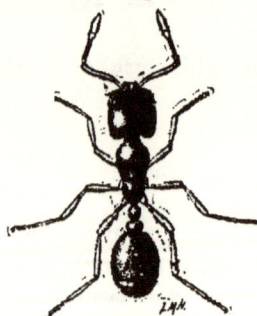

FIG. 1.—*Solenopsis molesta,*
worker; enlarged eighteen
diameters.

The first of these ants (Fig. 1) was
found by me abundant in many fields of
corn, both new and old, at Normal, Illinois,
in June, 1883, and at Champaign in May,
1886, where they were usually collected
about the kernels in the earth, and frequently more or less hidden in little cavities
excavated in the softened grain. May 19,
1887, they were very abundant in a field of
corn on sod in Champaign county, eating
out the planted kernels. In autumn the
same species has been detected by us
indulging a similar appetite, but in a way
to do no harm. September 11–21, 1893, it was found feeding on
and within kernels of corn at the tips of ears which had evidently
been injured previously by crickets and grasshoppers. The solid
substance of the grain is not actually eaten by these ants,—a fact
which I demonstrated by dissection of the ants,—but it is simply

Solenopsis molesta, Say (=*S. debilis,* Mayr).

gnawed away, doubtless for the sake of the sweetish and oily
fluids of the softened kernels.   If plants start from seeds thus
injured, they are shorter than those adjacent, and have a stunted,
weak appearance.

This species has also been several times noticed by us in September in attendance upon the root louse of corn, sharing with
several other species of ants the cares and benefits of this association.   It occurs more frequently, according to our observations,
at this season of the year, with the corn root lice infesting purslane than with those upon the corn itself.   I have also recorded in
my Thirteenth Report (p. 112) observations of injuries to ripe
strawberries by this house ant. •

The second species referred to
in this connection (Fig. 2) was seen
by us in Champaign, May 13, 1887, tear-
ing off fragments from a kernel of
sprouted corn just below the surface
of the soil, disposing of them much as
does the species mentioned above.
Many other grains were found in different parts of the same field similarly
injured, being sometimes, indeed, completely excavated.   The abundance
of this species and the obscurity of
the injury suggest that it may do
greater mischief than would appear
from this statement.

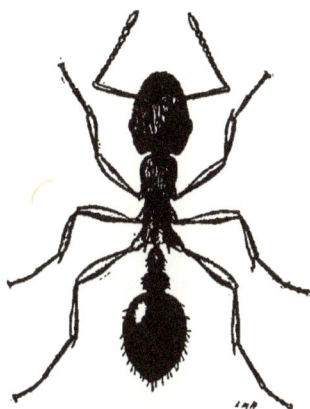

FIG. 2.—*Myrmica scabrinodis lobi-
cornis*, worker; enlarged eight
and one-half diameters.

This species, like the preceding, feeds in fall upon kernels of
corn at the tip of the ear in the field, most frequently following
injuries by other insects, but certainly sometimes hollowing out
the grain without their aid.

Its relations to the corn plant louse will be described in another
article.

2. *Injuries by small beetles* * *which gnaw away the kernel from
without, commonly beginning at the germ.*

Three common beetles have been detected by us and reported
by others as engaged in a somewhat noticeable injury to seed
corn in the earth, two of them among the most abundant of our

* Beetles commonly have four wings, the front pair of which are usually hard, thick,
and opaque, fitting more or less closely upon the hinder part of the body above, and
similar in appearance to the rest of the upper surface.   Beneath these, and next to the
body, may be found the membranous hind wings, generally entirely concealed except
during flight.   The segment bearing the hind legs is fixedly attached to the hind body,
but by a movable articulation.   They also have a biting mouth furnished with two pairs
of jaws.

Illinois insects, and the third also common, but too small to be noticed frequently by the ordinary observer.

The first of these is an oblong pale brown beetle (*Agonoderus pallipes*) with a blackish cloud on the back, from a half to a third of an inch in length and about a third as wide as long. It will be easily recognized by the illustration (Fig. 3). It is a species of common notoriety (although it has never received an English name) because of its annoying abundance at lights in early spring. Hibernating as an adult, it leaves its winter quarters with the first warm sunny days, and flies abroad at night in countless

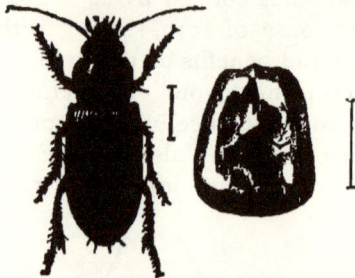

FIG. 3.—*Agonoderus pallipes*, imaigo; enlarged four and one-fourth diameters; its work in seed corn.

myriads. Shortly afterwards the eggs are laid in the earth, and a new generation comes forth abundantly in June and July. The adults themselves may be found, however, throughout the year. It is possible that more than one generation occurs in a season. We have noticed, in fact, a disagreeable abundance of these beetles at lights on warm September evenings. The species ranges throughout all, or the greater part, of the United States and Canada.

It was first made known to me as injurious to seed corn in the ground by a note from Mr. Thomas Huber, of Illinois City, Rock Island county, dated June 4, 1883, and accompanied by a specimen of the beetle "found in seed corn, buried in the kernel, eating the germ and part of the inside." In Bulletin No. 12 of the U. S. Department of Agriculture, Division of Entomology (p. 44), Professor Riley reports the receipt of this beetle during the summer of 1885, with the information that it was injuring young corn by gnawing into the seed and by eating the sprouting roots. One of these observations was confirmed by the sending of a specimen together with an injured grain. The exact amount of damage was not stated, but it was said to be quite extensive. Even before these observations I had myself detected this beetle injuring the roots of corn to some small extent;* a point determined by the dissection of specimens taken in corn fields, among the roots. Nearly half the food of these dissected specimens, however, consisted of fragments of chinch bugs, and other insect remains. The character and amount of this injury to corn have not heretofore been such as

---

*Twelfth Rep. State Ent. Ill., p. 43.

to call for protective treatment, but if the beetle should become sufficiently destructive to make such measures profitable, it is likely that "a satisfactory remedy will be found in soaking all seed corn for a short time before planting in some arsenical solution, such as Paris green or London purple, in water. Such a course will not injure the germinative quality of the seed, and will probably result in the death of all beetles which attempt to gnaw the seed."[*]

· The fact that a common small shining black dung beetle, *Aphodius granarius* (Fig. 4), very abundant in stable manure, where it feeds in part on fragments of undigested grain, may under favoring conditions transfer its attentions to seed corn in the hill, gives occasion for brief mention of this insect here.

Our only knowledge of this injury comes from Professor C. H. Fernald of the Massachusetts Agricultural College,[†] who received specimens of this beetle from Lancaster, Massachusetts, with the statement that they had been found destroying seed corn in the ground before it sprouted.

FIG. 4.—*Aphodius granarius*, imago; enlarged six and one-half diameters.

The third of these small beetles, *Clivina impressifrons* (Fig. 5), is included among insects injurious to seed corn upon the evidence of a single observation made by Mr. F. M. Webster in Indiana. He says: "I received from Whitly county, Indiana, a considerable number of these beetles, with the statement that they were found in a piece of ground which had been broken the preceding spring, the field being swampy and of a black soil, like those infested by wireworms. The beetles attacked the seed grains as soon as the latter became moistened. When received, one of the beetles had burrowed into a kernel of corn in the vicinity of the germ, and was engaged in devouring the substance."

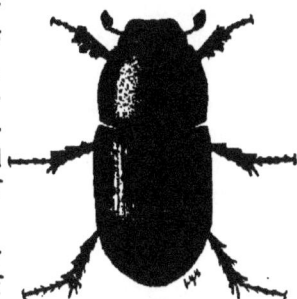

FIG. 5.—*Clivina impressifrons*, enlarged eight and one-half diameters.

*Bull. No. 12, U. S. Department of Agriculture, Division of Entomology, p. 45.
†Bull. No. 1, Hatch Experiment Station, Mass. Agr. Coll., p. 3.

3. *Injuries by footless maggots, which bury themselves in the seed grain.*

Two rather common injuries to seed corn in the ground are due to small white maggots without legs, one apparently headless, with much the form and general appearance of a very small blow-fly larva, and the other with a smooth, conspicuous head of a shining jet black color. The first is known as the seed-corn maggot, and infests corn only, as at present understood; and the second is the black-headed grass maggot, normally a grass insect, as its name implies, and injurious to corn only when this follows grass. Both these maggots penetrate the kernel, feeding on the mealy inner part, and leaving the outer shell. The first changes in the course of the summer to a small two-winged fly of the general form of the house-fly, and the second becomes a slender, small black gnat, roughly resembling the mosquito. The fly of the seed-corn maggot is little likely to be noticed in its winged state, but the gnat of the grass maggot is frequently seen in very large numbers on and near the ground in early spring.

THE SEED-CORN MAGGOT.

(*Phorbia fuscipes*, Zett.)

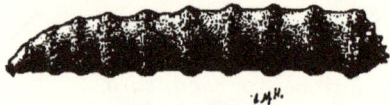

FIG. 6.—Seed-corn Maggot; enlarged eleven diameters.

This maggot penetrates the grain commonly after it sprouts but before it appears above ground, killing the germ or the growing shoot and finally hollowing out the interior so as to leave only the harder, outer parts of the kernel. In specimens of injured seed received by us from Altamont, Illinois, the larva had bored a round hole in the grain near the edge, and mined in a circular direction around the germ. In other grains it had entered at the tip of the germ, and in some beside the sprout. In one plant containing a full-grown maggot about two-thirds imbedded in the kernel, a root

about three inches long had formed, and a yellowish stalk had grown two inches in height. Still other grains had almost the whole interior eaten out. Unsprouted kernels, softened by lying in the earth, are also frequently penetrated in a way to destroy the germ. Commonly these injuries are trivial in amount, but in at least one instance mentioned by Dr.

FIG. 7.—Seed corn injured by Seed-corn Maggot.

Riley in his First Report as State Entomologist of Missouri (p. 154), the crop of a field in New Jersey was practically destroyed.   This insect is now known to attack not only sprouting corn in the earth, but also the roots of cabbages, radishes, onions, beans, and mustard, and the eggs of locusts (grasshoppers).

The adult is a small two-winged fly, about a fifth of an inch in length of body, not unlike a house-fly in general appearance, but smaller, and of a lighter form.   It is widely distributed, having been reported from Europe,—where it seems to have originated,—and also from Canada, New Jersey, and New York on the east, to Indiana, Illinois, and Missouri on the west.   Its life history is as yet incomplete, no continuous experimental work having been done upon it throughout the year.   Our miscellaneous observations and breeding-cage work give us thus far direct evidence of only a single brood, the maggots of which have been seen by us from May 17th to June 13th, the pupæ from June 7th to 15th, adults emerging from June 11th to August 7th.   It probably agrees with other species of its genus having somewhat

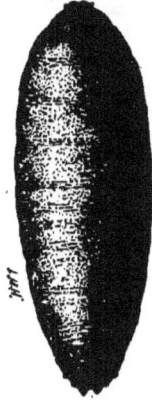

FIG. 8.—Pupa of Seed-corn Maggot; enlarged ten and one-half diameters.

similar habits in hibernating as a winged fly.   It is quite likely also that later broods appear, but not in corn.

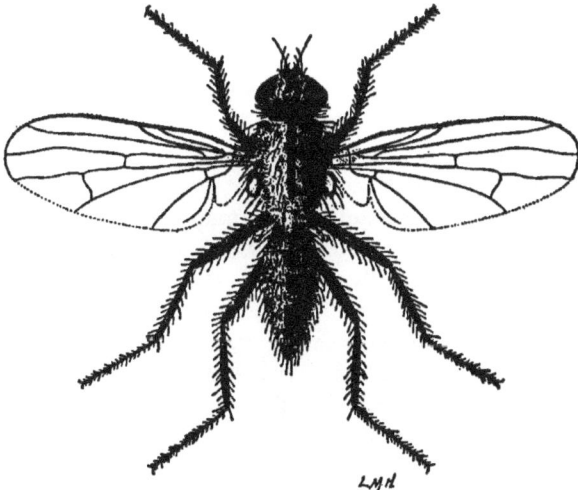

FIG. 9.—Fly of Seed-corn Maggot ; enlarged eight and two-thirds diameters.

THE BLACK-HEADED GRASS MAGGOT.

(Sciara, sp.)

When the spring is cool and wet after corn-planting, so that the softened seed lies long in the ground without sprouting, this is especially liable to certain kinds of injury; and it is under these conditions that the black-headed maggot seems most likely to affect it injuriously. Rotting grain is, indeed, undoubtedly preferred by this insect, but it has occasionally been seen to infest kernels which had begun to grow. It lives normally in old sod, feeding chiefly, or perhaps altogether, on decaying vegetation there, and will be found in noticeable numbers in corn fields only where the field was in grass the preceding year. These maggots penetrate

FIG. 10. and hollow out the kernel, often leaving nothing more than an empty hull. A score or more of them may infest a single grain.

They are also frequently noticed in rich garden ground and among potted plants, where they are accused by gardeners of eating the roots and hollowing out the bulbs.

They are slender, footless, white maggots (except that the head is jet black), about a third of an inch in length when full grown, and of nearly uniform diameter throughout. The body is soft and flexible, and the movements of the maggot are sluggish.

The species is very common throughout the State, and, doubtless, throughout the country at large, but it has been noticed in its relation to grass and corn only in an article in my Thirteenth Report (p. 57).

The larva was first brought to my notice as a corn insect in May, 1883, through Dr. Boardman of Stark county, who forwarded specimens to my office with the information that this insect was destroying newly planted corn in that county by eating out the substance of the germ, sometimes as many as three or four larvæ to a single kernel. The field had been a pasture previously—partly blue grass and partly timothy. Other fields of the neighborhood were abundantly infested, but only where the ground had been in grass the preceding year.

May 30, 1883, the same larva was observed at Towanda, McLean county, abundantly infesting corn on old sod, and other similar observations were made to July 10 of that year.

4. *Injuries by six-legged larvæ which gnaw or bore through the kernel.*

The six-legged insect larvæ which infest corn in the earth are of very unequal importance, the so-called wireworms being found more injurious to seed corn than all other insects taken together, the larva of the banded Ips being only occasionally reported to infest corn in the earth, and the other—that of the pale-striped flea-beetle—having been seen but once in this situation. Probably ninety-nine per cent. of the six-legged kernel-eating insect larvæ will be found to be wireworms of one or another species; and the greater part of these will usually belong, in Illinois, at least, to a single species which may well be called the *corn wireworm*. (See Fig. 26–29, p. 230.)

PALE-STRIPED FLEA-BEETLE.

(*Systena tæniata*, Say.)

Fig. 11.—Larva of Pale-striped Flea-beetle; enlarged nineteen diameters.

The larva of the pale-striped flea-beetle is a stiff, sluggish insect, slender and small, less than a fourth of an inch in length and about one-eighth as wide, dull, of a very pale yellowish color, minutely roughened and hairy, the thoracic segments with a regular geometrical pattern of longitudinal depressed lines. It is also distinguished by its peculiar form, which narrows noticeably from behind forward, the head being very small.

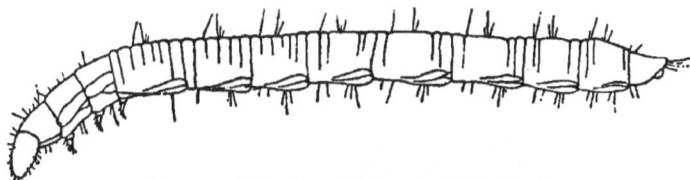

Fig. 12.—Side view of Pale-striped Flea-beetle.

In the only case in which it was found infesting growing corn (Champaign, May 17, 1886)* the larva had partly buried itself in the kernel beside the sprout. This and others of the species found among the roots were bred to the beetle stage on sprouting corn, pupating May 26th to June 7th and emerging as adults on the 17th of June. The great abundance of this insect in the beetle stage—so common as often to keep the leaves of the cockle-bur peppered with small holes where these beetles have fed—makes even so slight a hint of its capacity for mischief both interesting and im-

---

* See "Canadian Entomologist," 1886, Vol. 18, p. 177; "Entomologica Americana," Dec., 1886, Vol. II., p. 174.

portant. The adult insect also feeds on corn, as reported by
Glover on the authority of a correspondent, according to whom
these beetles nearly destroyed a field of corn at Chambersburgh,
Pa., eating the leaves and leaving the bare stalks standing. The
edges of the leaves may be gnawed away, sometimes nothing but
the midrib being left, or the leaf may be riddled with small holes.

The agricultural injuries of the beetle are not confined to the
corn plant, however, but it has been found by various entomologists to feed on beans, potatoes, beets,
clover, strawberry and blackberry leaves,
and the muskmelon, among useful plants,
and also on purslane, cockle-bur, plantain,
ragweed (Ambrosia), pigweed (Amarantus), and lamb's-quarters (Chenopo-
dium).

Beetles of this species have been
taken by us at frequent intervals from
April 8 to September 2, much the most
abundantly in June and July. Our substantial knowledge of its life history de-

FIG. 13.—Pale-striped Flea-
beetle; enlarged ten diameters.

pends, however, on the single breeding experiment already mentioned. Four larvæ were collected May 17, 1886, and placed at
once in breeding cages with sprouting corn. May 26th a pupa was
found lying on the earth in the cage. June 7th another pupa was
noticed yet in the earth, and on the 17th of June three adults had
emerged, and one pupa about mature was taken from the cage.

THE BANDED IPS.
(*Ips fasciatus*, Oliv.).

FIG. 14.--Larva;
enlarged eight
and one-third
diameters.

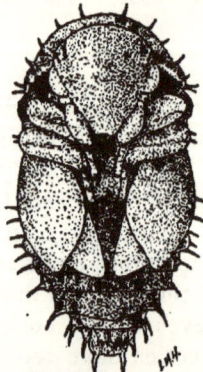

FIG. 15.—Pupa; enlarged
nine diameters.

FIG. 16.—Imago; enlarged eight
diameters.

Among the insects attacking the kernel in the earth, is the larva of a beetle, which in the adult state is abundant everywhere, feeding upon a great variety of vegetable substances, fresh or in a state of decay. The adult beetle has long been known as occasionally and slightly injurious to corn in the ear; but the fact that the larva may infest seed corn after planting, although first noted by us in 1883, has not hitherto been published.

My first observation to this effect was made at Normal, Ill., June 18th of the above year. In a field of corn a part of which had been in pasture for fifteen years preceding, while the remainder had grown turnips the year before—which, however, had not been removed from the ground—large numbers of these larvæ were found in and about the seed kernels.* From the first, stalks were growing fully two inches high. Occasionally a larva was seen in the space between the rows, but nearly all were concentrated in the hills of corn. Considering the ordinary habit of the species, it is quite likely that the beetles were attracted to this field by rotten turnips remaining in the ground.

June 16, 1885, larvæ were very abundant at Mt. Pulaski, in central Illinois, in the kernels of ears left in the field which had been turned under by the plow and had commenced to grow. May 16, 1887, a number were taken in a similar situation from a mass of sprouting corn at Urbana, Ill.

As an adult, this species was reported by Walsh in 1867, on the testimony of an anonymous correspondent, to have done an extensive injury some years before to sweet corn in Minnesota by burrowing in the ear; and Dr. John Hamilton, of Toronto, Canada, says that it is often found in the green ears of maize, but only in such as have been injured by birds or other animals. September 13, 1893, it was brought to my office by an assistant, Mr. Marten, with several injured kernels of corn, from the exposed tip of the ear, which the beetle had burrowed into or eaten away irregularly. In one other case reported under this same date it was found burrowing into doughy grains beneath the husk, more than an inch from the nearest exposed kernels, the natural inference being that the grains had not been previously injured. This very common species must consequently be classed as one of the minor insect enemies of corn, which it injures both as larva and adult—much more seriously, however, in the former stage.

The feeding habits of the larva are very much less known. Our own notes show, besides its occurrence in corn, that it breeds in rotten apples. The species appears from our observations to

---

* The field had been twice planted because of a partial failure of the first seed, and the kernels of both plantings were infested.

hibernate as an adult, and to give origin during the year to at least two generations. The larva enters the earth to transform, making a friable earthen cell.

WIREWORMS.

Failure of the seed to start, or a sudden withering of the corn plant when a foot or two in height, especially if the field was broken up from grass one or two years preceding, are always sufficient to warrant a suspicion of injury by wireworms. These hard, smooth, shining, reddish or yellowish brown cylindrical six-legged larvæ* are indeed much more destructive to seed-corn, under ground, in Illinois than all other insects taken together. They may begin their injuries to the seed almost immediately after planting, commonly burying their heads in it at first, sometimes eating entirely through the kernel, and even devouring it completely. If they attack the growing plant they are likely to eat the smaller roots, or to penetrate or bore through the larger ones, dwarfing or killing the corn; and later, when the young plant is several inches high, they frequently kill it outright by boring their cylindrical channels directly through the underground part of the stalk. They are far the commonest in corn on ground which has lain for several years in grass, and are much more likely to do serious mischief the second year after the breaking up of the sod. They should be sought for diligently on such lands whenever the seed fails to grow, or when the sudden withering of the plant hints at a serious damage to it under ground. At such times practically all the wireworms in the field will be found in the hills of corn or in their immediate vicinity, sometimes as many as ten or a dozen in each hill.

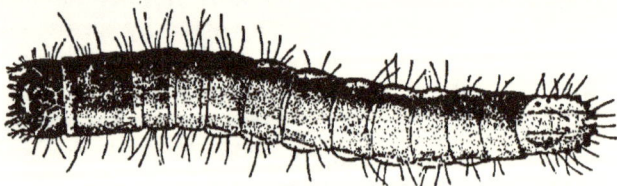

FIG. 17.—Larva of *Drasterius elegans;* enlarged seven diameters.

Although wireworms are rarely distinguished by farmers as of different kinds, there are no less than one hundred species of these insects known to occur in Illinois in the adult or beetle stage, and eight species of the larvæ (the so-called "wireworms" themselves) have been found by us here injurious to corn. These corn wireworms have, however, so strong a family resemblance that

---

*This general description of the wireworms does not apply to one very peculiar form (Cardiophorus), taken by us but once in Illinois.

they are little likely to be confused with any other insect by the fairly good observer who has once learned to recognize any one of them. They vary in length, when full grown, from half an inch to an inch and a quarter, but agree in their hard, crust-like surface, nearly destitute of hairs; their brownish color, varying from yellowish to reddish; their slender bodies, distinctly segmented, and of about equal diameter throughout their length; their flattened heads, with jaws borne in front and extending horizontally forward; the six pairs of short, stout, jointed legs on the three segments following the head; the absence of legs of any kind on the eight segments thereafter; and the single sucker-like proleg on the under surface of the last segment of the body—the thirteenth, counting the head as one. This terminal segment is often peculiarly finished above—concave or convex, notched, toothed, or lobed at the sides and end, or, in one species, with a pair of conspicuous round openings on the upper surface. Taken in the fingers, the wireworms bend and wriggle with surprising strength, and easily slip out of the grasp.

They live regularly and normally in grass lands, feeding on roots of grass, where, however, their numbers are rarely sufficient to produce any notable effect upon the sod. It is only when concentrated in the comparatively scanty vegetation of a field of young corn in spring, or occasionally in young wheat or other small grain, that they do any very marked or important harm. They are to be found in grass of every description, from prairie sod and the coarse and rank sedges along the borders of marshes, to the cultivated grass of our pastures and meadows.

The commonest form of attack on the corn, as seen by the farmer, is, perhaps, the burrowing of the worm into the seed kernel, either before or after it has sprouted. All the species treated in this paper have been seen with their heads buried in the kernels,

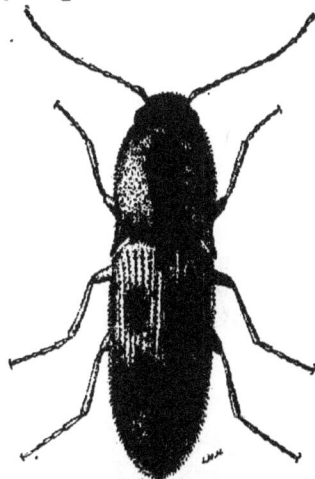

FIG. 18.—*Drasterius elegans*, beetle; enlarged seven and a half diameters.

either in the field or in breeding-cages. Frequently attacks in the field have been so severe, particularly the first or second year after the sod has been broken, as to require planting a second or third time. *Drasterius elegans* (Fig. 17 and 18) and *Melanotus fissilis* have been taken in the act of perforating stalks just above the root. In a field at Peru, Illinois,

examined July, 1883, as much as six per cent. of the corn in the
field had been killed in this way, sometimes two or three larvæ
being found in a single stem.

FIG. 19.—Cardiophorus sp., larva, dorsal view; enlarged four diameters

The roots of the corn are also eaten to a greater or less extent
by all the species, the damage from this cause being sometimes
quite considerable. .A field in Alexander county visited in June,
1886, had spots of one hundred to two hundred hills not more than
a foot high, while the balance of the field was four or five feet
high. Many hills in these spots were gone. In the smaller hills
many small, slender, peculiar-looking larvæ of an unknown species
of Cardiophorus were found. (Fig. 19.) In some instances they
had almost•completely destroyed the roots of the corn; in others
the roots were bored through and the outer surface eaten away so
as to almost destroy their usefulness.

FIG. 20.—Wheat Wireworm; enlarged five diameters.

Agriotes mancus is so destructive to wheat as to be known as
the "wheat wireworm" (Fig. 20, 21, and 22). *Drasterius elegans*
is also known to infest this crop, as do other species as well. Rye,
barley, and oats also suffer from wireworm attacks. Dr. Fitch
also found them burrowing in timothy bulbs. Wireworms taken
from a dense clover sod and placed in our breeding-cages, where
they were supplied only with grass and clover, gave us imagos of
Asaphes decoloratus. (Fig. 23, 24, and 25.)

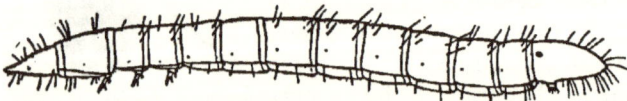

FIG. 21.—Side view of Wheat Wireworm.

Among root crops, potatoes often suffer from being bored into
and by having the surface gnawed and corroded by the worms;
but turnips, it is said, appear to be more infested by them than any
other root crop.

Besides the crops already mentioned Dr. Fitch names the following, which the wireworms are known to attack or are recorded
as attacking: mangel-wurzel, cabbage, carrots, beets, onions,
lettuce, rape, hops, strawberries, pinks, carnations, dahlias, lobelias,
and numerous other garden flowers. They have also been reported
to me by a horticultural friend as destroying planted peach pits in
the earth.

GENERAL STATEMENT OF LIFE HISTORIES.

The injurious species agree fairly well in the main features of
their life history, changing to the dormant pupæ in the earth in
July or sometimes in August, and changing again some three or
four weeks later to the brown or
reddish beetles commonly known
as "click beetles" or "jumping-
jacks"—hard, somewhat hairy insects, of slender oval form, distinguished at once by their peculiar
habit of springing into the air with
a sudden click when placed upon
their backs. A large part of these
fully developed beetles remain under ground until spring, enjoying
there the protection of the oval
earthen cavity or cell formed by the
larva as a preparation for pupation.
A part, however, come forth from
the ground in fall, passing the winter
in sheltered places, and the remainder emerge in spring, laying

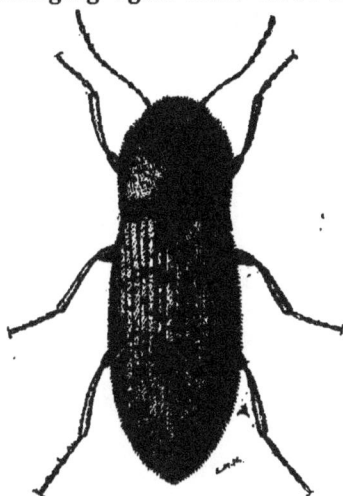

FIG. 22.—Beetle of Wheat Wireworm;
enlarged seven diameters.

their eggs most commonly in grass lands in the earth. Of their
subsequent life history little is yet definitely known. It seems
certain that all live more than one year as wireworms in the earth,
and observation of the various sizes of larvæ of the same species
to be found in the field at once, usually supports the common impression that the period of life in the larval stage does not extend
beyond two years; a fact which, taken in connection with the
death and decay of grass roots the first year after breaking up the
sod, serves to explain the greater damage done by wireworms the
second year the ground is in corn. The number of wireworms
having been little diminished since the crop was changed, and
their original food having practically disappeared, they are com-
pelled to concentrate upon the corn—either the newly planted seed
or the young plant while it is still very small.

NATURAL ENEMIES OF WIREWORMS.

Only a single parasitic fly has been bred by us from wireworms. Comstock and Slingerland frequently found them killed in their breeding-cages by a fungus determined by Professor Roland Thaxter as probably *Metarrhizius anisopliæ.* Those killed by this disease have the body filled by the growth of the fungus, and assume a woody appearance. An Asaphes larva turned out by the plow at Champaign May 10, 1886, was infested by a parsitic fungus of another genus, very much like Cordiceps.

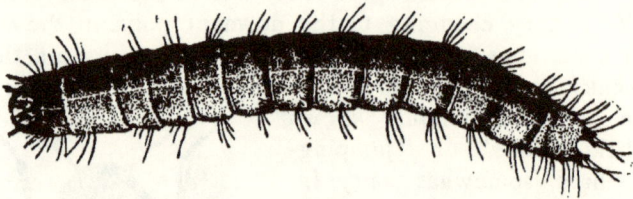

FIG. 23.—Larva of *Asaphes decoloratus;* enlarged three and three-fourths diameters.

· In my work on the food of birds,[*] I found that some seventeen species eat to some extent "click beetles," or their larvæ, the wireworms. These insects constitute about two per cent. of the food of five species of the thrush family—the robin, and the brown, the hermit, the wood, and the Alice thrushes. The examination of the food of these birds continued throughout the year, and the proportionate amount of these beetles eaten was found to be greatest during the months when they were most numerous; but even then the quantity destroyed was scarcely sufficient to affect materially their average numbers. Mr. E. V. Wilcox,[†] while studying the food of the robin, at the Ohio Agricultural Experiment Station, found in the stomachs of twenty-seven of these birds, shot in April and May, "click beetles" amounting to three and one-half per cent. of their food. Of the remaining species of birds known to eat them, none take enough to make more than a fraction of one per cent. of their food, except, perhaps, the crow. Dr. Fitch says that "wireworms and their progenitors, the snapping beetles, constitute the favorite food and principal sustenance of these birds [crows]."[‡]

[*] Bull. Ill. State Lab. Nat. Hist., Vols. I and II.
[†] Bull. Ohio Agr. Exper. Station, No. 43, (1892), p. 127.
[‡] Eleventh Rep. (Trans. N. Y. State Agr. Soc., (1866), p. 542.

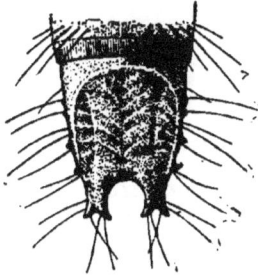

FIG. 24.—Last segment of
larva of *Asaphes decoloratus;*
much enlarged.

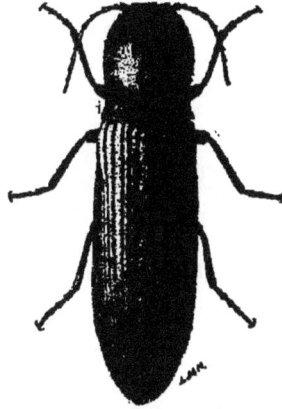

FIG. 25.—Beetle of *Asaphes
decoloratus;* enlarged four and
a fifth diameters.

PREVENTION AND REMEDY.

Probably no class of agricultural insects has had prescribed for
it a longer list of artificial remedies than the wireworms, and certainly no such list has been of less practical value.   After many
generations of experience with their work in this country and in
Europe their injuries continue at present practically unchecked by
any treatment consistent with the methods of American agriculture.

Even poisons of the most deadly sort applied to corn previous
to planting, or to food lures distributed through the ground for the
purpose of drawing off the attention of these insects from corn,
have proved almost entirely valueless, both in my experience and
in the more elaborate trials made by Comstock and Slingerland in
New York.   Late fall plowing, breaking open the pupal chambers
within which the recently transformed adults pass the winter, will
probably have the effect to diminish generally the number of
these beetles during the following year.   Comstock and Slingerland have also ascertained that the adult beetles are susceptible to
certain poisons judiciously distributed with certain attractive kinds
of food ; and I have to suggest a systematic rotation intended to
interpose between grass and corn a crop not vulnerable to the
wireworms.   Otherwise we are substantially without a hint of any
means of diminishing the ravages of these insects other than the
time-honored resource of the corn farmer, namely, late planting of
his corn the second year after sod, and late replanting if the first
planting is destroyed.   In the latter case it is well to plant between
the rows, allowing the first corn to stand as long as is consistent
with a proper cultivation of the field.   All the wireworms being at

the time concentrated in the old hills of corn, if these be destroyed when the field is planted the second time, the wireworms still active in the earth are forced to attack the freshly planted kernels as their only food resource.

FIG. 26.—Corn Wireworm; enlarged four diameters.

The first experiments with poisons for the wireworms of which we have definite record, were made at my office in 1885, and reported briefly in my "Miscellaneous Essays on Economic Entomology" (p. 18), printed the following year.

FIG. 27.—Side view of a middle segment of Corn Wireworm.

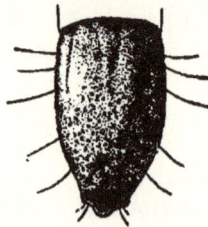

FIG. 28.—Last segment, dorsal view; greatly enlarged.

FIG. 29.—Beetle of Corn Wireworm; enlarged four and a half diameters.

Later, in May, 1888, we fed thirty-seven wireworms on corn soaked for seven days in a mixture of water and Paris green. The corn was covered with a coating of the green poison, and was eaten freely by some of the worms without killing them. Twelve wireworms fed on corn soaked in Fowler's solution diluted with an equal quantity of water were not affected, although a portion of the corn was eaten. Twelve others, fed on corn soaked in an alcoholic solution of arsenic, were not injured by the poison, though feeding freely on the corn. Experiments in June and July, when wireworms were fed on corn soaked in a solution of arsenic in boiling water, were less satisfactory because the larvæ were so near pupation that they ate little or none, pupal cells being formed five days after the experiment began. Corn soaked in a solution of strychnine—four grains to a half pint of water—over night, and fed to seven wireworms June 28, 1888, had not affected them by July 5th, although the corn was slightly eaten. Twelve worms supplied with corn soaked twenty-four hours in an alcoholic solution of corrosive sublimate June 27, 1888, did not eat the corn.

A repetition of these experiments in June and July, 1891, by a different assistant and under somewhat different conditions, gave substantially the same results.   June 27, 1891, corn was soaked in a saturated solution of potassium cyanide and fed to three wireworms.   July 3d one grain of corn was slightly eaten, and July 10th one grain was badly eaten and one worm missing—probably eaten by mice that had obtained access to the cage. July 20th several grains were badly eaten; July 27th the remaining two worms were active, but the corn was untouched; and the experiment ended without effect.

In many of the experiments, particularly when alcoholic solutions were used, or where the corn was soaked for a considerable length of time in arsenical solutions, it failed entirely to germinate ; while in experiments where the grain was simply wet and rolled in the arsenites, or soaked for only a few hours, it grew almost as freely as did untreated corn in check lots.

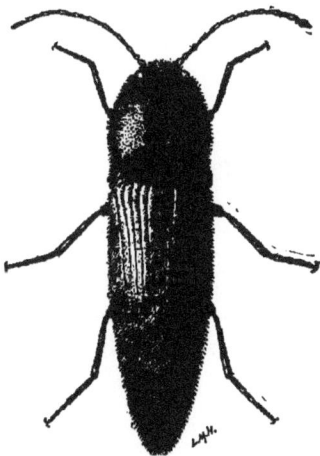

FIG. 31.—Side view of a middle segment of larva of same species, showing muscular impression, spiracle, etc.

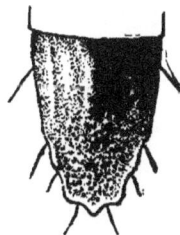

FIG. 30.—Beetle of *Melanotus communis;* enlarged four diameters.

FIG. 32.—Last segment of same, dorsal view ; greatly enlarged.

These experiments with the arsenical poisons and strychnine agree substantially with those of Messrs. Comstock and Slingerland, published in November, 1891, and show that it is not practicable to protect the corn by means of them, even were it possible to use them without retarding or preventing the germinating of the seed.

Coating the kernels with tar and soaking them in a solution of salt, a solution of copperas, a solution of chloride of lime and copperas, in spirits of turpentine, and in kerosene oil, have been tried by Comstock and Slingerland without encouraging results.

Applications of kerosene emulsion and pure kerosene made to the worms in the earth were found by me in 1885 practically ineffective, any strength sufficient to kill the larvæ killing vegetation also. Similar results were obtained by Comstock and Slingerland, who, after using crude petroleum, an emulsion of the same, and a common kerosene emulsion, concluded that the last is more promising than the others, but that it cannot be profitably applied on a large scale. Experiments made by them show also that even a clean fallow for an entire season will not starve out the worms; that neither buckwheat, mustard, nor rape crops—frequently recommended to clear the earth of wireworms—will accomplish the desired result; and that salt applied at the rate of 1,600 pounds to the acre—a heavy dressing—neither drives the wireworms deeper into the soil nor causes them to migrate to any appreciable distance; that kainit used as a fertilizer, even in very large quantities, had little effect if any on the wireworms;* that muriate of potash—four to six tons to the acre (an excessive amount)—is but slightly effective; that lime at the rate of even two hundred bushels per acre does not injure wireworms; that chloride of lime must be used in impracticable quantity to produce any marked effect; and that gas-lime, although capable of destroying the wireworms, must be applied in such great quantities that its use is impracticable on large areas. Bisulphide of carbon poured into a hole in the earth near the infested hill destroys the wireworms, but at an excessive cost.

The most promising remedy for wireworms, in my judgment, is one which has unfortunately not been experimentally tested,

---

*These results are inconsistent with those reported by Prof. J. B. Smith in the 12th Ann. Rep. N. J. Agr. Exper. Station (for the year 1891), p. 412. Here Professor Voorhees, Chemist of the Station, is said to have applied kainit and muriate of potash separately to two sections of a fourteen-acre piece of corn on ground always badly infested by wireworms and cutworms, leaving a strip between these sections without treatment. Care was taken that the sections should be similar with respect to quality of land, situation, etc. As a consequence, the kainit section was reported as almost entirely exempt from injury by insects, the muriate section as but little infested, and the intermediate strip as almost destroyed. It is evident from the context that this experiment had been made some years before, apparently not under the inspection of an entomologist.

but which is, nevertheless, precisely based upon our knowledge of the life history, food, and habits of these insects. It consists of a rotation in which clover follows always upon grass and is itself followed by corn. According to this plan pastures and meadows of grass might lie unchanged for several years, being plowed, when broken up, in late summer or early fall and sown to clover in the spring—either with oats, or on winter wheat or rye sown the fall before. The clover should be allowed to stand a second year, and might then be followed with corn with positive assurance that the wireworms originally in the sod would by that time have entirely disappeared. From the regular rotation for grain lands, grass would be thus excluded. In such a rotation corn might be followed by small grain, this by clover, and this by corn. While the wireworms might produce some visible effect on the small grain the first year after grass, this would usually be much less serious, at any rate, than the damage to corn.

The general entomological effect of some such management could not fail to be beneficial, since it would apply to cutworms and white grubs as well as to the wireworms now under discussion. The system of rotation now common in central Illinois is, indeed, seriously defective in the fact that the plants composing it—Indian corn, small grains, and grasses—are all of the same botanical family and consequently subject in large measure to the same enemies. Any variation of this system which will introduce as a regular link in the chain a crop belonging to some other and widely different family of plants, will serve the general purpose of that here proposed.

B. DETAILED DISCUSSION OF INJURIES TO THE ROOTS.

Injury to the roots of corn in spring and early summer may be indicated to the close observer by the aspect of the growing crop. If the corn fails to appear in spring, the difficulty may not be due to poor seed or to injuries to the kernel, but may be caused by an early insect attack upon the young roots, which may even kill the plant outright before the sprout has broken ground. The root louse of the corn and the wireworms are most likely to be concerned in this form of injury.

Later in the season, when the plant is a few inches high, the uneven growth of the corn will often attract attention, patches here and there advancing slowly in comparison with parts of the field adjacent, and in a way not to be accounted for by differences of soil. In such cases, white grubs, wireworms, corn-root worms, or plant lice should be sought for. Combined with this uneven growth, or possibly in times of drouth without it, the farmer may notice yellow patches in his field, the color being most pronounced upon the lower leaves. The root louse of the corn will be found responsible in most cases for this partial discoloration, but any of the species just mentioned may produce a similar effect,* or it may be caused on the lower part of the stalk by the chinch bug.

An especially significant symptom of more or less serious mischief is the presence in the field of numerous burrows of ants, commonly placed in or immediately near the hills of corn, and most conspicuous shortly after rains. This invariably indicates the presence of root lice in the field, although if the corn be small a careful search may fail to detect them at the time. The nature of the association between the ants and the root lice is such that the former prepare the way for the latter early in the season by sinking their burrows among the corn roots, thus giving the lice access to them.

If at about the time the ear is beginning to form, and from that time onward, the stalks of corn are easily prostrated by wind and rain, and do not readily rise again, it will commonly be found that the hold of the plant upon the earth is abnormally slight, so that the hill may be pulled up too easily. This condition of the plant is due to a loss of roots, usually to be attributed to one of the corn root worms, or, more rarely, to the white grubs. Sometimes, however, a similar appearance is given late in the season to a field infested by the chinch bug, which by abstracting sap from about the base of the stalk just beneath the surface of the ground will often prevent the shooting forth of the so-called "brace-roots," which serve to anchor the top-heavy stalk more firmly in the earth.

------

* A condition of the corn very similar to that just described is not due to insect attack at all, but, as is supposed, to a bacterial disease of the roots known as the *corn root blight*, fully described by Prof. T. J. Burrill in Bulletin No. 6 of the Illinois Agricultural Experiment Station (August, 1889). In this disease the corn stops growing in patches, becoming yellow and usually slender, and sometimes dying while young. The yellow color is most pronounced upon the lowest leaves. On pulling up the plant, the oldest and the lowest roots are seen to be injured and usually dead, the bottom part of the stalk to which these roots are attached being similarly affected. If split through the middle, the inner tissue of this lower part is seen to be of a uniform darker color, and a slight discoloration, becoming less and less pronounced above, appears in the next succeeding joints, while the parts between them are seemingly healthy. On the surface, when carefully cleared of dirt, brownish corroded spots may be found, sometimes covered with a firm gelatinous material.

1. *Some of the roots deadened, hardened, or dwarfed, without loss of substance.*

   a. Small brown or yellowish ants abundant in the hills, and very small, bluish green or whitish, oval, thick-bodied, root lice on the larger roots.

PLANT LICE AND MEALY BUGS.

(APHIDIDÆ AND COCCIDÆ.)

Associated with ants in hills of corn, the observer may find any one or more of eight species of minute, soft, thick-bodied, six-legged insects, sometimes winged, but usually without wings, and always of very sluggish habit and slight power of locomotion. When exposed, they may show little or no signs of disturbance, but if shaken off the roots into which their stout jointed beaks are thrust, they will probably crawl slowly and clumsily about, making movements almost too sluggish and aimless to look like efforts to escape. The ants which have nested in the hill will, however, commonly seize these little insects in their mandibles and hurry away with them into concealment.

By far the greater part of those answering to the above description to be found in the corn field, will usually be plant lice (aphides); and will mostly belong, in fact, to a single species, the corn root aphis; but a few may be "mealy bugs" (genus Dactylopius, family Coccidæ), recognizable as such by their general resemblance to the kinds of "mealy bugs" common in greenhouses. They may be readily distinguished from the plant lice by their thicker, clumsier bodies, and by the almost rudimentary size of their legs and antennæ. They are always covered with a mealy or powderly excretion of minute particles of wax, and never have honey tubes, or cornicles, on the back of the abdomen—both, however, characters in which they agree with some of the lower plant lice. From all the corn-infesting plant lice they may be technically separated by the fact that their tarsi are single jointed, and bear but a single tarsal claw, while the plant lice of this group have two tarsal joints and a pair of tarsal claws.

Plant lice are among the most prolific of insects,* producing several generations annually, but they are commonly held severely in check by climatic, meteorological, and biological conditions; that is, by season, weather, and plant or animal parasites. They

---

*Slingerland has bred twenty-five generations of a plant louse (*Myzus achyrantes?*) in a single year (Science, Vol. XXI., 1893, p. 48); and Buckton shows (A Monograph of British Aphides, Vol. I., p. 80) that a single rose aphis (*Siphonophora rosæ*) might give origin, at its normal rate of unchecked multiplication, to over thirty-three quintillions of plant lice in a single season, equal in weight to more than a billion and a half of men.

are, consequently, capable of rapid and enormous increase when
any of these checks are temporarily weakened to any considerable
degree. As they affect the plant by abstracting the elaborated
sap upon which its vital activity depends, the injury done is usually
general, and especially is this true if the root be the part infested.
Some species, however, in addition to this general drain upon the
life of the plant, cause a distinct local deformity to root or leaf in
the nature of a gall, which protects them at the same time that it
secures them food. Any crop liable to their attack in force is
never long free from danger, but, on the other hand, a seemingly
irresistible outbreak may disappear as quickly as it came, a slight
and almost imperceptible change of conditions often taking tre-
mendous effect on these delicate insects.*

Economically, plant lice may be divided, according to the
peculiarities of their life histories, into several groups or classes.
Some generation, or some part of some generation, may grow
wings, fitting them for rapid dissemination, or the species may be
without winged representatives. They may live through the whole
season of their active life above ground, on exposed parts of the
plant; they may spend the whole season under ground, upon the
roots; or they may alternate, spreading each year from roots to stalk
and leaves and back again. Whatever part of the plant they infest,
they may live on a single host species, they may spread indefinitely
from one to several others, or they may migrate definitely, by
means of a fixed generation, from one species to another, requir-
ing thus for their continuance two plant species often extremely
unlike.

Finally, the sexual, oviparous generation (commonly the last
to appear in fall) may leave its eggs on the exposed parts of the
plant last infested, or it may deposit them in the earth among or
on the roots of its host. In the former case the destruction of the
plant, or of its remains, will destroy the lice; in the latter, the
eggs rest like a seed in the earth to stock the ground the following spring with a horde of young, ready to infest the succeeding
crop if suited to their tates and habits.

All the plant lice of our present list of species infesting the
roots of corn are, so far as known, subterranean only, producing
no galls, but leaving their eggs in the earth over winter. They
infest more than one plant, spreading from one to another species
in an indefinite manner, not definitely migrating. The corn and
grass root lice. (*Aphis maidiradicis* and *Schizoneura panicola*)

---

*A marked illustration of this fact is afforded by the somewhat recent history of the
grain louse (*Siphonophora avenæ*) in Illinois. (See Seventeenth Report State Entomologist of Illinois, p. X.)

develop early in the season winged forms by which they easily spread from field to field.

Six species of plant lice, belonging to as many different genera, have been found by us habitually infesting corn roots in Illinois. By far the most important of these is that commonly known as the corn root aphis. This is, in fact, the only one on the list which infests corn primarily as a principal food plant, the others being essentially species of the meadow and pasture, attacking corn but lightly, and most commonly only when it follows grass.

The association of all these species with ants, which care for them in many ways, some of them indispensable, and feed in turn on excretions of their insect charges, is a fact of special economic significance, since the ant most active in preserving the plant-louse species must be taken into account as a factor in the economic problem.

THE CORN ROOT APHIS.

(*Aphis maidiradicis*, Forbes.) ·

(FIG. 33 — 37.)*

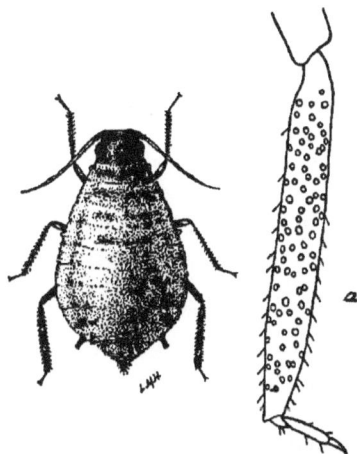

FIG. 33.—Corn Root Aphis, oviparous female; enlarged fourteen diameters: *a*, hind tibia, showing sensoria.

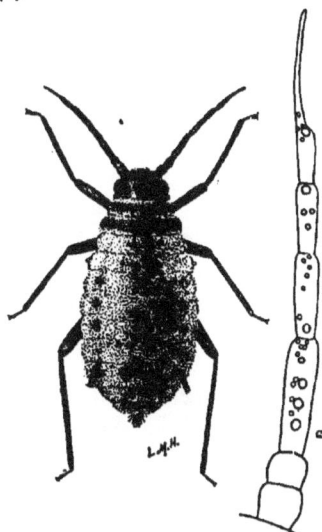

FIG. 34.—Male of same species; enlarged twenty-five diameters: *a*, antenna.

No insect affecting corn is more deserving of the attention of farmers and entomologists at the present time than the corn root aphis. It ranks as a corn pest with the chinch bug and the army

* A colored plate of the oviparous female, and of winged, wingless, and pupa forms of the viviparous female of this species, was published in the Seventeenth Report of the Illinois State Entomologist.

worm, less injurious at any one time than these are locally and occasionally, but overtaking them, on the other hand, by its general distribution and the constancy of its attack. Although it lives upon the roots throughout the life of the plant, the principal damage is done at the same time as that caused by wireworms— while the corn is still small. It contrasts with the corn root worms with respect to the time of its most injurious activity, the latter coming in at about the time when the aphis generally begins to loosen its hold; but the two agree in the fact that they make their first appearance in spring only on ground which has been in corn for at least a year preceding.. The common root worm is confined throughout the season to the field in which it hatches, while the aphis presently scatters abroad, more or less freely according to the percentage of the second and succeeding generations which develop wings. On the other hand, although its worst mischief coincides with that of the wireworms, it is not commonly the case that both are especially injurious in the same fields, the wireworms following grass of the first and second year preceding, and the plant louse most commonly infesting corn on old corn ground only. As lands recently in grass are most likely to contain the white grubs also, it is not a common thing to find the corn root aphis early in the spring in grub-infested fields.

Its life history is now probably very well understood, but thoroughly effective remedial measures, I regret to say, are not yet certainly known. Rotation of crops will often greatly decrease or even prevent injury by dispersing the attack, but we have no conclusive proof that this measure diminishes to any considerable extent the number of root lice in the country during any one year. It is therefore probable that this insect is increasing slowly in average numbers from year to year, and it may yet bring serious disaster to agriculture throughout the whole region best adapted to the culture of Indian corn.

Although I have no data for a precise account of its distribution, it has been recognized by us in all parts of the State from Cairo to the extreme northern limit, and has been definitely reported outside Illinois, from Maryland, New Jersey, Indiana, Ohio, Kentucky, Minnesota, and Nebraska. It is altogether likely that it occurs in larger or smaller numbers throughout the whole corn belt.

FIG. 35.—Corn Root Aphis, wingless viviparous female; greatly enlarged:
  a, apex of abdomen showing cornicles, tubercles, and cauda.

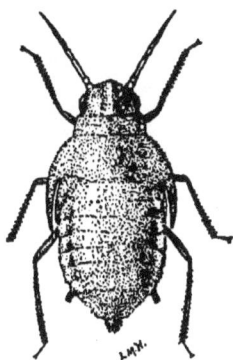

FIG. 36.—Pupa of same species; enlarged twenty-one diameters.

INJURY TO CORN.

The corn root louse is a suctorial insect, taking only fluid food
through a stiff beak, which it thrusts into the tissues of the plant
it feeds upon, producing thus no external injury, nor, indeed, any
local internal effect discoverable by ordinary methods of observation.   Indications of injury by this insect are consequently all of
a general character, affecting the entire plant, and do not materially differ from those caused by severe drouth, except in the fact
that they are likely to be unequal in different parts of the same
field in a way to indicate no connection with the amount of re-
tained moisture in the soil.

A noticeably greater abundance in early spring in the lower
parts of an infested field seems to be due to the greater abundance
there of young weeds on which the corn root aphis feeds at first.
As soon as the corn starts to grow it may become infested, and
even be killed outright before it appears above ground.   We have,
in fact, found the root louse on the plant as early as May 9th, only
four days after the field was planted.

The dwarfing of the plant, especially in patches here and there,
with a yellowing or reddening of the leaves—beginning of course
with the lowest ones—and a general apparent lack of thrift and vigor,
are sufficient to cause suspicion of injury by this louse, a suspicion
which will be confirmed in part if numerous burrows of ants are
seen in or near the hills of corn.   The presence of ants in the field
may be overlooked after the ground has been recently cultivated,

but can scarcely escape attention shortly after a rain, when these little insects actively open up their burrows, heaping up the little pellets of earth about the openings of their nests.

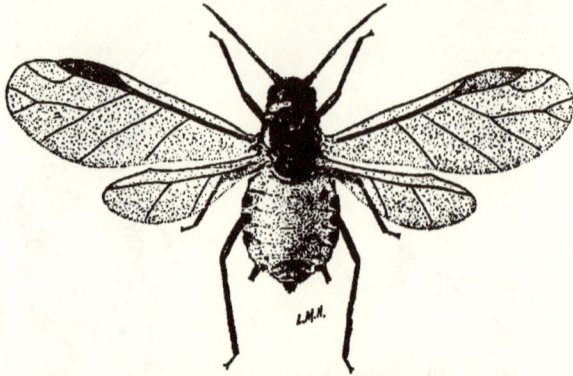

Fig. 37.—Winged viviparous female of Corn Root Aphis;
enlarged sixteen diameters.

The appearances described may, nevertheless, be due either to the corn root blight—a disease not caused by insects, and hence not treated in this report—or to the grass root louse, a species likewise attended by ants, but far less injurious to corn than the aphis under discussion. If the damage be due to the root blight, the root lice themselves will be few or wanting; and if to the grass louse, the fact may readily be ascertained by an examination of the roots of the corn.

The root aphis of the corn is of a bluish green color, slightly whitened by a waxy bloom. The form of the body is oval, and on the hinder part of the back are two short, slender, but conspicuous, tubes, standing erect or projecting slightly backwards, which may be seen by the glass to have open ends externally. These are called the cornicles of the aphis, or, sometimes, the "honey tubes," it having been formerly supposed that they were the source of the abundant excretion upon which the ant attendants of the lice eagerly feed. The grass louse (Fig. 40 and 41), on the other hand, is white in color, with a blackish head and other blackish markings, but without any tint of green; and it has no trace of cornicles, their place being taken by two minute openings in the corresponding segment of the body, each surrounded by a delicate brownish rim.

The evidences of serious injury by the corn root aphis are, in short, an unusual dwarfing and discoloration of the corn, an abundance of small brown ants in the field, nesting among the hills, and, finally, the presence of the bluish green insects themselves upon the larger roots of the corn, especially near the base of the stalk.

The amount of injury may vary from a scarcely noticeable check upon the growth of the plant to a total destruction of the corn over considerable patches, up to half an acre or more. This more serious effect is, however, rarely, if ever, produced by the root louse alone. Like most insect enemies,—especially those of suctorial habit, which abstract the sap of the plant they feed upon,—the corn root aphis serves to intensify the effect of drouth and other unfavorable influences, and it is often difficult to say how much is to be ascribed to the action of the insect pest and how much to other causes coöperating.

There is some evidence to the effect that a too serious check to the growth of the corn results in the early evolution of a great number of winged plant lice of the second spring generation, whose escape from the fields in which they start so breaks the force of the attack that in a favorable season very badly damaged plants may rally and make good corn; but if the insect injury is followed or reinforced by drouth, the corn may grow sluggishly the whole season through, and either fail to ear, or bear small imperfect nubbins only. Sometimes a field not infested the year before is permanently damaged·in June, or even late in May, as the result of an early accidental concentration of the winged lice originating in other fields.

INJURY TO OTHER PLANTS.

No other crop plants are especially liable to injury by this aphis, unless possibly we should except broom corn and sorghum. Although not at all uncommon on these plants, it does not commonly thrive on them, and so far as my observations have extended, can scarcely be called injurious to them. It has been observed in the field, however, or bred in the insectary, on the roots of a number of other species of plants, some of which are, in fact, important to its maintenance. Many of the first generation hatch from the egg in the field before the corn is ready to receive them, and at this time young smartweed plants and foxtail-grass (Polygonum and Setaria) are their principal resource. These plants harden early and lose the succulence which makes them especially desirable to plant lice, a fact which accounts in part no doubt for the early transfer of the lice to corn; but in fields of small grain, Setaria and Polygonum may continue to support the corn root louse at least until the second generation is well matured. Indeed, I have found this insect on the roots of smartweed more than a foot high as late as June 17th. Crab-grass (Panicum) also becomes infested, but less abundantly than the Setaria, and from the latter part of June throughout the rest of the season the aphis breeds abundantly on the common purslane (*Portulaca oleracea*). We have occasionally found it so abundant on purslane plants far removed from corn fields—beside paths in lawns and in other similar situations—that one might well regard this as a purslane aphis, if it were not for the fact that this weed starts too late in the season to serve as food for the earlier generations.

We have, further, experimental evidence that the corn root aphis can live on roots of ragweed (Ambrosia), having transferred May 8, 1889, half-grown young of the second generation from smartweed roots to this plant, where they lived and fed until they acquired wings, five days later. The fall oviparous generation and the one preceding it have been repeatedly reported by my field assistants—who were constantly dealing with the root aphis and knew its characters perfectly—to have abundantly infested dock (*Rumex crispus*), fleabane (*Erigeron canadense*), mustard (*Brassica nigra*), sorrel (*Oxalis stricta*), plantain (*Plantago major*), Hungarian grass (*Setaria germanica*), pigweed (*Amarantus hybridus*), and squash; but as these statements were not verified by successful transfers from these various plants to corn, they rest only on determinative evidence, notoriously unreliable with respect to the plant louse species. Indeed, an attempt at transfers of the supposed corn aphis found on squash, sent me from Ohio by Prof. C. M. Weed, entirely failed. A similar result was reached in an attempt to transfer known corn root lice from corn to wheat and oats, begun April 22d, 1889. Insects placed on roots of wheat in breeding-cages April 22d continued to live there until May 5th, but without producing young. May 11th, however, all had left the plants. An earlier experiment, begun April 10th, had a like ending, and a precisely similar result was obtained in a parallel experiment with oats.

The repugnance of this insect to the roots of small grain was repeatedly shown also by field observations. Fields of oats and wheat on old corn grounds, sometimes known to have been badly infested by the root aphis the preceding year, often contained in April and May large numbers of these root lice and their associated ants, the former feeding on the roots of smartweed and pigeon-grass growing with the grain, but never being seen on the roots of the grain even where these and the grass roots were closely interlaced.

The relation of this louse to other plants than corn has an important economic bearing. For example, in fields on old corn ground, the first generation of plant lice are very noticeably more abundant early in spring in the lower parts of the field than elsewhere, especially in those parts so situated as to receive the wash from the remainder. I can at present only account for this unquestionable fact by the very much greater abundance here of young smartweed plants, doubtless due to the washing down of the seeds left on the ground in fall. This seems especially likely to be the true explanation, since the difference in the number of plant lice on low and high ground in the same field diminishes greatly or entirely disappears with the advent of later generations and the scattering of the winged lice abroad.

LIFE HISTORY.

General Statement.—The corn root aphis passes the winter as an egg in the earth, in corn fields or, rarely, in other grounds where purslane grows late in fall, always, so far as known, only in the nests of a small brown ant about an eighth of an inch long, known to science as *Lasius niger* or its variety, *L. niger alienus.* This ant is the constant companion of the root louse throughout the year, living in burrows among the roots of the corn. The aphis eggs begin to hatch about the· time of the opening of the seed leaves of the smartweed or heartweed (*Polygonum persicaria*), abundant in cultivated ground. This first of the spring generations is readily distinguished by characters of form and color from all that follow. Appearing usually before the corn is planted, it is dependent at first, in our region, almost wholly upon the young smartweed plants. The roots of these are laid bare by the burrows of the ants, and upon these roots, within their narrow tunnels, the lice will usually be found thickly clustered. Later, if the field be not planted to corn, our common species of pigeon-grass (Setaria) divides the attention of the lice, offering in fact, for a little time, a more succulent herbage than the rapidly growing smartweed.

The second generation begins to appear about the 1st of May, —we have one breeding-cage record of the 28th of April,—and by the middle of that month may be itself mature. Many of this generation are winged, while others are without wings,* the winged form first occurring about May 10th.† These "migrant" root lice may live at first, like those of the preceding generation, upon smartweed and pigeon-grass, but more commonly they are transferred to corn by the little brown ant already mentioned, either in the same field or after they have flown to another. These ants not only carry from weeds to corn the root lice already in

---

*Two young of this generation, born of the same mother in a glass tube enclosing a corn root, were kept by us until adult, when one proved to be a wingless aphis and the other winged.

†This generation is at its best from May 15th to 20th in average years in central Illinois.

their possession, but burrow hills of corn in advance, eagerly seizing and conveying to their subterranean galleries winged root lice which come their way.

The succeeding generations are not of special economic interest with the exception of the last to occur—the autumnal, bi-sexual brood, by which the eggs are laid. Both males and females of this brood are wingless, and live in the earth like their parents, occurring there from the middle of September to the middle of November. The eggs which they lay are taken in charge by their attendant ants and cared for during the winter.

Number of Generations.—The eggs of the corn root louse begin to hatch as early as April 10th, this process continuing, according to our observations, until May 2d. Our numerous breeding-cage experiments, although not one of them is continuous throughout the year, enable me nevertheless to give a fairly full account of the number and succession of generations. According to these the first three generations have an average life of nineteen days, while the fourth to the twelfth follow each other at an average interval of about eleven days. Many of our observations show that a much earlier start and a more rapid growth are common, and that a greater number of generations may consequently occur.

No special attempt was made to determine the number of individuals a single female may produce or the relative productiveness of the various successive generations. The fact is however worthy of record that a single stem mother placed on a corn root in a breeding cage May 4th, brought forth her first young May 6th and her *twelfth* and last May 15th. At this time the first-born was a pupa, acquiring wings on the 19th. The stem mother lived until the 22d, and was then placed in alcohol. Another female of a midsummer brood brought forth fifteen young.

According to the results of experiments conducted for the purpose of determining the number of moults of the corn root aphis, and the intervals between successive moults, we find that this species moults four times, at average intervals of three or four days. Our most successful observations upon this and several other nice points of individual life history were made on isolated specimens, each placed upon the root of a potted plant which was then passed through a small glass tube and covered with earth except where the tube enclosed it. To prevent the escape of the plant louse the ends of the tube were lightly plugged with cotton-wool.

Migration to Uninfested Fields.—The last autumnal brood of the corn root aphis lives, so far as known, only upon roots of corn and purslane, the latter being usually infested in corn fields only, and in these situations, consequently, the eggs are left from which young hatch the following spring.* This first spring generation being always without wings, the root aphis is practically confined for a little time to fields previously in corn. As a considerable part of the second generation acquires wings, a general dispersal of adults begins almost as soon as the corn is out of the ground. These winged root lice do not, however, become sufficiently abundant for a considerable time thereafter to noticeably affect fields not in corn the year before. Previous to the first of June this distributed attack can scarcely be detected, and not until July 1st have we found it really serious anywhere.

The evolution of winged root lice is not confined to any single generation, but continues throughout the season in numbers varying according to some law not yet ascertained. It is to be noticed, however, that we have taken the winged form in August but once, although our collections of wingless specimens were made on twenty-seven days within that month. In September also the winged louse is relatively rare, occurring but three times in twenty collections made on as many different dates. By November the viviparous generations are all dead, as a rule, and the species is thereafter represented only by the sexual generation and the egg.

RELATION TO ANTS.

Seven kinds of ants have been found by us fulfilling the relation of host, guardian, and nurse to the corn root aphis. The occurrence in this relation of all but two (*Lasius niger* and *Lasius niger alienus*, Fig. 38 and 39) is so rare that they need receive here no more than this passing mention, especially as their services to the aphis are, so far as observed, the same in character and value as those of the much more abundant species.

The fact has already been mentioned in this paper that the sexual egg-laying generation of the corn root aphis—the last to appear in fall—is born in the galleries of the nests or homes of ants, and that here the sexes pair and the females drop their eggs. As one explores these nests in November, when the root louse eggs are being laid, he is struck with the relative independence of these oviparous adults, which are allowed to wander unattended through the burrows of their hosts as far as a foot or more from a corn root. We have found them, however, still feeding as late as November 5th, and laying eggs November 21st. These eggs, which are yellow when first deposited, but soon become shining black,

---

*Among more than fifty lots of "stem mothers" of the corn root aphis collected by us in the field, every one was found in ground which had borne corn for at least the year immediately preceding.

and turn green just before hatching, are at first scattered here and there, as it happens, but are finally gathered by the ants for the winter in little heaps and stored in their galleries, or sometimes in chambers made by widening the gallery as if for storage purposes. If a nest is disturbed, the ants will commonly seize the aphis eggs —often several at a grasp—and carry them away. In winter they are taken to the deepest parts of the nests (six or seven inches be-, low the surface in some cases observed) as if for some partial protection against frost; but on bright days in spring they are brought up, sometimes within half an inch or less of the surface, sometimes even scattered about in the sunshine, and carried back again at night—a practice probably to be understood as a means of hastening their hatching. I have repeatedly seen these ants in confinement with a little mass of aphis eggs, turn the eggs about one by one with their mandibles, licking each carefully at the same time as if to clean the surface. These anxious cares are of course explained by the use the ants make of the root lice, whose excreted fluids they lap up greedily as soon as the young lice begin to feed. They are not, however, wholly dependent on this food supply, at least in early spring, as I have seen them kill and drag away at that season soft-bodied insect larvæ, doubtless to suck their juices out as food. This has been a somewhat rare occurrence, however, and has rarely been noticed by us among ants which had plant lice in their possession. Once, however, ants of this species occurring abundantly in corn fields were observed September 22d to carry bits of dead insects into their burrows, together with a living corn root louse.

That the young of the first generation are helped by the ants to a favorable position on the roots of the plants they infest is quite beyond question. It is shown (1) by the fact that in many cases the aphis could not get access to such roots unless these had been previously laid bare by the tunneling of the ants, and (2) by the behavior of ants with mines already constructed, when the root aphis is offered to them. We have repeatedly performed the experiment of starting colonies of ants on hills of corn in the insectary and exposing root lice from the field to their attentions, and in every such instance, if the colony was well established, the helpless insects have been seized by the ants, often almost instantly, and conveyed under ground, where we would later find them feeding and breeding on the roots of the corn. In many cases in the field, we have found the young root aphis on sprouting weeds (especially pigeon-grass), which have been sought out by the ants before the leaves had shown above the ground; and, similarly, when the field is planted to corn, these ardent explorers will frequently discover the sprouting kernel in the earth, and mine along the starting stem and place the plant lice upon it.

We have also abundant evidence that ants excavate hills of corn in very early spring, when they have as yet neither eggs nor plant lice in their possession, and some days before the possible appearance of the second or winged generation. I can only account for this practice on the supposition that these ants expect later to obtain eggs or young with which to stock their burrows, made ready in advance. Certainly this is true with respect to the second generation of the root aphis. When winged lice of this brood begin to appear, it is a common thing to find the small brown ant scattering far and wide over fields not previously in corn, and containing consequently no plant lice in any stage, burrowing there the hills of corn, and carrying underground such corn root lice as come within their range.

I need hardly say that the relations above described between the corn root aphis and these ants continue without cessation throughout the year, the succeeding generations being quite as useful to the ants as those whose history I have thought it worth while to follow in detail.

NATURAL ENEMIES.

Although various insect species, mites, ground beetles, and the like, have been found in more or less suspicious relation to the corn root lice in our breeding-cages, and even in the fields, no known case has occurred with us of destruction by an insect enemy. It is, indeed, a remarkable fact that not a single hymenopterous parasite has ever been bred from the corn root aphis in all our long experience with that insect. It is true that root lice are much less parasitized than those feeding in more exposed positions, but they are nevertheless by no means commonly free from parasitic attack.

The only natural check upon the increase of this root aphis which has come immediately to our notice is a parasitic fungus, *Entomophthora fresenii*, detected October 16, 1889, infesting sexual individuals of this species found on roots of the curled dock (*Rumex crispus*) at Champaign, Illinois. Affected specimens were of a creamy or whitish color, and were literally crammed with the small oval granular spores of the Entomophthora.

ECONOMIC PROCEDURE.

Our present knowledge of the life history of the corn plant louse suggests four possible methods of attack. (1.) We may try the effect of a change of crop after any notable plant-louse injury to corn, in the expectation that corn planted on ground which contains no plant-louse eggs will become so slightly or so slowly infested, if at all, that no harm need be anticipated. (2.) We may resort to fertilizers and other applications made to the young corn hill in spring in the hope of killing the lice outright or of supporting the plant against their attack at a time when this is likely to be most injurious. (3.) Since the small brown ant cares assiduously for the eggs in winter and spring, we may assume provisionally the necessity of such care and strive to find means of so disturbing the nests of the ants or of breaking up and dispersing their contents in late fall or in winter that their stores of aphis eggs cannot be recovered by them, and so shall be left to perish. (4.) Taking account of the early hatching of the eggs in spring—several days, as a rule, before the usual time for planting corn,—and the dependence of the young lice for food at that time on sprouting weeds in the field,—especially smartweed and pigeon-grass,—we may seek to handle the ground in such a manner that there shall be no sufficient start of vegetation to keep the lice alive. We may also delay somewhat, if necessary to this end, the planting of the field to corn.

Rotation of Crops.—There can be no doubt that a judicious rotation of crops has the effect at least to diminish injury by the corn plant louse by distributing its attack; and there is also considerable reason to believe that it must result in the destruction, direct or indirect, of a certain proportion of the insects themselves. Corn planted on ground not previously stocked with plant-louse eggs must escape at any rate until invaded from without by winged individuals of the second generation, and then, as a rule, it will be no more subject to injury than the other fields in its neighborhood. On the other hand, as the corn root aphis has never been known to infest to an injurious extent any other crop following corn, there is very little probability that the escape of the corn will be balanced by damage to other crops.

We have many observations going to show that wheat and oats and the smaller grass-like plants in general are commonly soon deserted by such corn root lice as commence to breed on them—a fact which indicates that these plants are less suitable than corn to the maintenance and multiplication of these insects. We have also considerable reason to believe that many winged plant lice flying about in search of feeding and breeding grounds must be destroyed by some of the innumerable accidents to which these feeble and helpless insects are necessarily exposed. This measure of rotation may consequently have the effect to diminish to an important extent the number of corn root lice in later generations. Precise proof on these points is, however, very difficult to secure. Artificial breeding experiments are altogether too variable in result to serve the purpose, as our own attempts at a solution of this question show; and evidence must be sought in the field especially by making detailed comparative observations of parts of the same previously infested fields, planted here to corn and there to small grain. The relative abundance of the lice late in May and early in June will go far to show the comparative utility of these crops as a food resource to the corn root aphis.

Applications of Fertilizers and Insecticides.—Various field observations have given us reason to conclude that fertilization of the soil will serve to support corn under the drain of aphis injury, especially by enabling a stunted plant to rally more rapidly and completely after the insects have begun to scatter. The rapidity and vigor with which, in rich ground and in a fairly favorable season, corn will outgrow an apparently fatal injury by the root aphis is, in fact, often quite surprising. Apart from this general statement I have only to report the result of a single series of plat experiments tried in 1891 with various fertilizers mingled with petroleum, crude and refined, as an insecticide, and with applications of salt, wood ashes, and lime.

A plat of ground ten hills square, containing ninety-seven hills of corn, was selected on the University experimental farm at Urbana June 18, 1891, and surrounded by a continuous line of six-inch boards sunk about three inches into the ground, with close-fitting joints, and with the earth well tramped both outside and in. The upper edge of the boards was thickly covered with coal-tar, subsequently kept fresh by repeated applications. These measures were intended to prevent all interference with the experiment, either by escape of the insects within the plot or by invasion from without. June 26th this enclosure was enlarged to contain twenty-three hills more. Fertilizers, and mixtures of fertilizers and petroleum, were applied to the hills of corn June 18th and 23d, being worked into the soil about each hill; and on the 26th lime, ashes, and salt were similarly applied. Of the ninety-seven hills in the first enclosure, forty-eight were found in the beginning to contain root lice and ants, and of the twenty-three hills in the second lot sixteen were similarly infested.

Three fertilizers were applied: superphosphates, muriate of potash, and sulphate of potash, each at the rate of three pounds to twenty hills of corn, and in each case half the hills under experiment were treated with the pure fertilizer and the other half with a mixture of fifteen ounces of petroleum to three pounds. One-third of the above amounts were applied June 18th,—the petroleum in these cases being the crude Lima oil,—and the remaining two-thirds, June 23d, when refined petroleum was used. The following notes are condensed from the memorandum filed at the time by the assistant* in charge of the experiment:

Experiment I., Superphosphates.   Experiment II., Superphosphates and Petroleum.

June 29, I.   Ants and root lice numerous.
"   29, II.   Both insects present but less numerous than in I.
July   1, I.   Ants and lice abundant.
"   1, II.   Ants present but no lice.
"   7, I.   Ants and lice abundant.
"   7, II.   A few ants but no lice.
"   15, I.   Ants and lice comparatively abundant.
"   15, II.   Ants and lice both present but fewer than in I.

Experiment III., Muriate of Potash.   Experiment IV., Muriate of Potash and Petroleum.

June 29, III.   A few ants and lice found.
"   29, IV.   Dead plant lice discovered in one hill, both ants and lice occur-ring generally but not abundantly.
July   1, III.   A few ants but no lice.
"   1, IV.   Ants alone discovered on roots about one foot from the hill, just outside the fertilized area.
"   7, III.   Ants and root lice found.
"   7, IV.   Ants but no lice.
"   15, III.   Ants plentiful; lice common.
"   15, IV.   Few ants and lice detected.

Experiment V., Sulphate of Potash.   Experiment VI., Sulphate of Potash and Petroleum.

June 29, V.   Ants present but no lice.
"   29, VI.   A few ants present but no lice.
July   1, V.   Neither ants nor lice were found.
"   1, VI.   A few ants and lice in one hill.
"   7, V.   Ants and lice numerous.
"   7, VI.   Both insects present.
"   15, V.   No ants or lice detected.
"   15, VI.   Small colony of ants and a few lice in one hill.

The weather during the period covered by the above experiment was generally dry, but abundant rains occurred June 20th and 21st, which seemed to dissolve the fertilizers and wash them into the ground.

The lime, ashes, and salt experiments were entirely without effect, ants and plant lice occurring abundantly in all parts of the plat treated throughout the entire period of observation to July 28th. This plat served consequently as a check upon the preceding experiment.

Although the effect of the other applications seems from the above notice to be quite marked, the experiment is nevertheless indecisive, since the hills treated were not dug up when examined from time to time, but only searched as carefully as was possible

---

*Mr. J. S. Terrill. The work was, however, done under the immediate supervision of Mr. John Marten, one of my present entomological assistants.

without injuring the plants. July 28th, when all the hills were removed, they seemed, according to Mr. Marten's report, to be about equally infested, all appearance of difference having then vanished. It will thus be seen that these experiments have little value except as hints towards future work. The differences observed may nearly all have been due to a repellent effect of the substances applied, in consequence of which the ants withdrew their charges deeper into the earth, with little diminution perhaps of the injury to the corn.

Breaking up Nests of Ants.—In one experiment, begun November 25, 1890, a strip of corn stubble three rods wide and ten rods long near the University premises at Champaign, was plowed six inches deep, half the strip being thoroughly harrowed also. The ants' nests among the corn hills were thus turned out and thoroughly broken up, except that in a few cases the plow did not go the full depth of the nests, but left the bottom undisturbed. The harrowing knocked the dirt out of the roots of the corn and broke up the fragments of the nests remaining in the clods. April 18, 1891, when the ground was again plowed, five ants' nests were found in this plat and thirteen in an equal strip beside it. All of these outside nests contained ant larvæ of various sizes, while those inside the strip contained no ants but worker adults. Ten of the former lot of nests and three of the latter contained root lice also, on smartweed roots.

In another precisely similar experiment, begun upon the same day in an adjoining field, a strip was plowed two and a half rods wide by twelve rods long, half of this being thoroughly harrowed, as before. The plowing averaged six inches in depth, but the plow ran considerably deeper under the corn rows, and the ants' nests were well broken up and scattered. April 17th of the following spring the ground was plowed for corn and thoroughly examined to determine the result of the experiment. The part which was harrowed contained three ants' nests, the remainder six; while on an equal strip adjoining, thirty were found. None in the strip plowed in fall contained young ants, while every one of those outside contained them. Several wingless females were seen in the nests, one of them in the plowed strip.

Neither the weather at the time nor that of the following winter was especially favorable to the success of such an experiment, the mercury reaching a maximum of 49° F. on the day the experiment began, and the winter following—that of 1890-91—being unusually open and warm. Further, there had been more than a week of warm spring weather previous to April 18th, the mercury reaching 72° on the 9th, 75° on the 13th, and 77° and 78°

on the 17th and 18th respectively—temperatures at which ants as active as the little *Lasius niger alienus* might well disperse themselves and begin new colonies in unoccupied ground.

These experiments afford, perhaps, scarcely a sufficient basis for a final conclusion as to the economic value of this method, but so far as they go they are most encouraging. If we compare the treated plats with the check plats beside them, we find (1) that the ants' nests in the former were less than a third as many as in the latter; (2) that all in the plowed and harrowed plats were destitute of ant larvæ while in the check plats all without exception contained such larvæ; and (3) that in the single plat first mentioned the ants' nests containing lice were less than a third as numerous as those in the plat outside.*

From the above we can only infer the disastrous effect of this late fall and winter plowing upon the ants themselves, and, presumably, also upon the plant louse eggs they have in charge. It seems also quite probable that some, if not all, of the nests found April 18th in the experimental plats had been established there by worker ants in spring, and were not remnants of the nests previously broken up, and if this were the case the root lice found in them had doubtless been brought in from without.

Starvation Experiments.—April 15, 1889, twelve young root lice recently hatched were placed in a cavity in the moist earth, which was covered with a glass slip so placed as to allow an examination of the interior.   April 20th two of these root lice died; the next day half the lot were dead; April 22d only two were living; April 23d but one; and on April 24th, nine days from the beginning of the experiment, all were dead.

May 14, 1888, a number of corn root lice of various ages, taken from the roots of young smartweed in the field, were placed in a glass vial with moist earth, the mouth of the vial being covered with gauze. On the 18th all were still alive, but by the 20th all had died, the earth in the vial still remaining moist.

April 30, 1890, a number of eggs were placed in a cavity in sterilized earth and left to themselves. May 1st one young louse appeared from the only egg of the lot which hatched, and May 3d this one was dead.   It appeared from the foregoing that young of this species hatching in the earth and kept without food would die in from two to nine days.

As a field application of this fact, an attempt was made April 16, 1889, to starve the young lice in the ground by keeping down the growth of young weeds. A piece of ground was thoroughly

---

* By an unfortunate oversight no mention was made in the notes on the second experiment, of root lice in either the plowed strip or check.

harrowed in two directions with a cutaway disk harrow, and the weedier parts of the plot, several times additional. April 20th, however, ants and lice were found both within and without the harrowed strip; but the ants had no plant-louse eggs in their possession where the ground had been harrowed. The result of this treatment was not especially encouraging, the young weeds sprouting so freely and abundantly in the moist earth, to a depth of four or five inches, that it seemed impossible to reduce the food supply of the lice to any considerable extent by mechanical methods.

Our present knowledge of effective economic procedure for the corn root aphis may be summarized in the form of the following recommendations: (1) that the fertility of the ground should be maintained as a general safeguard, and that cultivation should be so managed—especially that of the lower parts of the field—as to prevent so far as practicable the seeding of pigeon-grass and smartweed among the corn; (2) that infested fields should be plowed deeply and thoroughly harrowed late in fall or during some suitable early winter interval; and (3) that a somewhat rapid rotation of crops should be systematically followed, corn usually being allowed to grow on the same ground but two years in succession.   While some work remains to be done with reference to the precise value of these methods in practical application, there is no longer any doubt of their substantial usefulness, at least as a means of holding in check the injuries of the corn root aphis.

ON THE ANTS ATTENDANT UPON THE CORN ROOT APHIS.

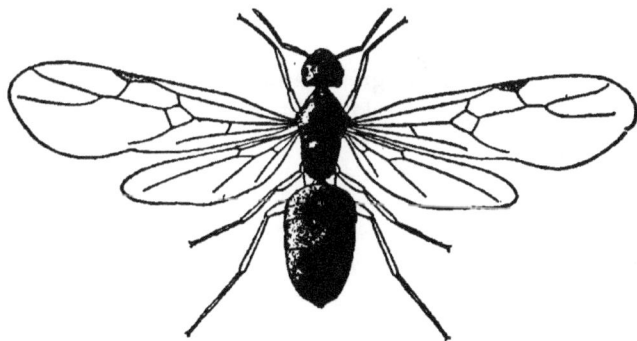

FIG. 38.—Small Brown Ant (*Lasius niger alienus*), female ; enlarged four and a half diameters.

Lasius niger and its variety *alienus* are so far the most abundant of the seven species of ants which we have found in attendance upon the corn root aphis that a discussion of the economics of this relation need scarcely take account of any other species; but as the most promising protective measures against this aphis are based on our knowledge of the life history and habits of this commonest corn-field ant, an accurate account of the latter is to be desired. Our notes on this subject cover the entire period since 1883, and enable me to give a fairly complete history of this species throughout the year.

Life History.—The winged sexual forms, male and female, of this ant begin to appear each year as early as the latter part of June (the 21st to the 27th), hatching from pupæ which may have formed late in May (27th and 28th, by our notes). The emergence of males and females from the pupa continues throughout the season, certainly into October and probably to November, but the males perish before the winter. The females, however, having been fertilized and deprived of their wings, begin their separate excavations in fall, or continue with the workers in nests already established. There they hibernate, sometimes at least, commencing to lay their eggs in fall, and living in spring through April and May.

We have found the eggs of this species only November 10th, April 25th, and May 20th; but exceedingly small larvæ certainly very recently hatched have been collected by us May 5th to 19th, July 15th, and September 21st. Our experiments have not, however, been conducted in a way to distinguish between eggs and young coming from fully developed females and those from fertile workers.

The larvæ hatching from time to time throughout the summer may be found as pupæ from the latter part of May through June, July, August, and September, to October 30th, and even, according to a single observation made at Urbana, to November 20th.

Haunts, Actions, and Habits.—The nests or burrows of this ant, in which these breeding operations are carried forward, are

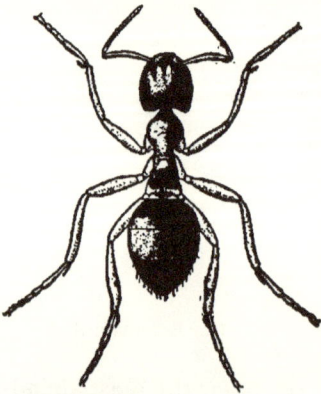

FIG. 39.—*Lasius niger alienus*, worker; enlarged eight and a fourth diameters.

widely distributed in corn fields and grass lands,—especially in the latter, along the borders of roads and paths, —and also under stones and boards, in and under decaying logs, and in an indefinite variety of situations. In corn fields they are established almost wholly in the hills of corn, and remain here among the old corn roots throughout the season. As this is the commonest and most generally distributed of all our ants in Illinois, an exhaustive list of its places of habitation would have little present interest. It has never been found by us to form large settlements, or making mounds or conspicuous structures of any kind; but simply scatters its little burrows almost indiscriminately, living in small families rather than in great colonies or city-like aggregations, and piling up only a small temporary heap of pellets around the mouth of its burrow. When its mines are explored they are found to consist of irregularly radiating and connected tunnels, rarely going to a greater depth than six or eight inches, or extending outward over a horizontal area of more than twelve or fifteen inches. Here and there in their course or at their extremities and at various depths are chamber-like enlargements in which their eggs and young and the eggs of the corn root aphis are preserved and cared for. Here also considerable collections of the worker ants are usually found,—especially in winter. and in times of summer drouth,—and in these chambers the female resides and lays her eggs.

In April, May, and June the workers seem to be most numerous and active. In July and August their activity declines, particularly in the hottest and dryest weather, although if nests be opened at these times the ants will be found in abundance. Again, in September, a period of bustling activity begins which continues until checked by the winter cold.

In ordinary winter weather of the milder sort, these ants are not absolutely motionless, but if disturbed crawl slowly and stupidly about, sometimes even painfully attempting to perform their usual duties of restoration and repair. We have not explored their nests in the coldest weather, when the ground is frozen to a considerable depth.

During the first warm days of spring the thoroughly awakened ants begin to open up their burrows to the surface, and carry their own eggs and young and the eggs of the plant lice in their possession upwards and downwards according to the varying warmth of different layers of the soil. When the sun is shining brightly in the middle of the day they bring their charges to the more superficial chambers of their nests, or even expose them on the surface, but keep them farther downward at night and in cold and cloudy weather. The effect of this care upon the plant-louse eggs is shown by the earlier hatching of those cared for by the ants, and by the diminished number of those which fail to hatch at all.

Although this ant is evidently chiefly dependent for food upon the corn root aphis and other plant lice fostered by it, it is not strictly limited to this resource but, early in spring especially, has been found by us with freshly killed insects in its possession —caterpillars, carabid larvæ, and the like. Sometimes in midsummer also it resorts to animal food. July 16, 1884, in digging into a hill of corn infested by the root aphis and this ant, I unearthed a carabid larva. This was suddenly attacked by one of the ants, which pounced upon it just behind the head. The larva struggled vigorously, but the ant soon fastened its jaws on the under side of the neck, just behind the head, and a little to one side of the middle line. After this the struggle lasted only a few seconds, when the larva became completely quiet, and allowed this ant and another to drag it away without the least resistance. I watched this operation for a few minutes with a glass, and then put both ants and larva into alcohol. Although the larva did not visibly bleed when bitten, it was apparently dead, and did not struggle at all when put into alcohol.

June 2, 1891, an ant of the above species (*Lasius niger*) was found with a dead chinch bug in a wheat field, and three others were seen dragging live chinch bugs over the ground, one of which bareley showed signs of life, a second of which moved its legs more vigorously, while a third, which an ant was dragging along by the beak, seemed scarcely at all disabled.

THE GRASS ROOT LOUSE.

(*Schizoneura panicola*, Thos.)

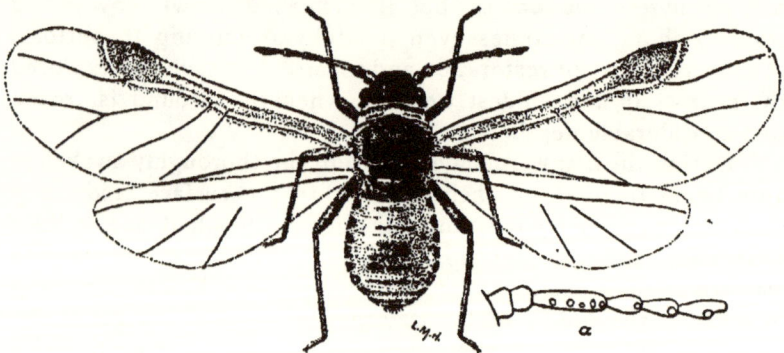

FIG. 40.—Grass Root Louse, winged viviparous female; enlarged eighteen diameters: *a*, antenna.

This species was discovered on the roots of *Panicum glabrum* and other grasses by Mr. H. Pergande, at St. Louis, Mo., in November, 1877, and first described by Dr. Thomas in 1879 in the Eighth Report of the State Entomologist of Illinois. The first observations of its occurrence in this State on corn were made in 1883, and it has been seen by us more or less abundant on the roots of various plants every year during the past eleven years. Its economic importance is but small, owing to the usually trivial

numbers in which it occurs on corn, and the evanescent character
of its attack.   It is often important, however, that the corn farmer
should be able to distinguish it from the far more dangerous corn
root aphis—a matter of no difficulty to a fairly good observer.   It
may be told at once from that species by its white or yellowish
color, and by the absence of the projecting cornicles or honey-
tubes characteristic of Aphis, these being replaced in the present
species by a pair of minute circular openings on the hinder part of
the back, each delicately rimmed with brown, and surrounded by
a small dark patch.

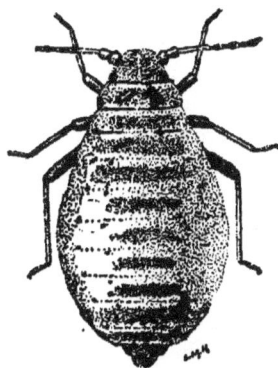

FIG. 41.—Grass Root Louse, wingless viviparous female ; enlarged 29 diameters.

2. *Roots evidently injured or destroyed by perforations, gnawing,
   burrowing, decay, or other loss of substance.*
   a.   Roots eaten away, not burrowed or perforated, and with-
        out rotten or withered tips.   Tap-root commonly gone
        or decayed.   White grubs in soil among or beneath the
        roots.

THE WHITE GRUBS.

GENERA LACHNOSTERNA AND CYCLOCEPHALA.

(FIG. 42–47.)

White grubs or "grub worms" are among the immemorial
enemies of agriculture on both sides of the Atlantic, and in both
Europe and America the problem presented by their injuries on
the farm and in the fruit and vegetable garden still calls for
thoroughgoing investigation and scientific treatment.   In fact,
the steady increase of their numbers in this State—probably connected with the gradual enlargement of the area laid down in grass
—has made such an investigation of their life histories, habits, and
economic relations simply imperative and indispensable.

They infest a great variety of plants, nearly all of which have
an agricultural value, many of them being the great staple crops

of the farm and garden. Grasses of every kind, all the small grains, Indian corn, potatoes, beets, and the root crops generally are liable to destruction by them, as well as strawberries and young fruit trees, young evergreens, larches, and young forest trees of various kinds.

Like most other injurious insects of the first class, they are liable to great variation and fluctuation of numbers in different localities and in successive years, sometimes getting the temporary mastery of a considerable tract, appropriating nearly its whole growth of vegetation to their own use, and then, within a year or two, disappearing from view for a time as an injurious agency. Apart from these seemingly spontaneous fluctuations of numbers, they are most likely to cause great loss when the crop on ground infested by them is changed by rotation from one affording them an abundance of food to one yielding a relatively scanty growth—as when grass lands are planted to corn. A number of grubs which would produce no visible effect in a dense sward, may be sufficient to devour completely a field of young corn.

They hatch most commonly in grass lands (although frequently also in corn), from eggs laid there by various kinds of beetles, all commonly confused under the general name of "June beetles" or "May beetles" or "dor-bugs." These large, thick, short, snuff-brown beetles, a half inch to more than three-fourths of an inch in length, nearly as thick from above downwards as they are wide, and about half as wide as long, are universally known because of their great abundance in May and June, during which months they fly at night, filling the air at dusk with their hoarse buzzing, and often invading lighted rooms in our houses, where they bump and bumble about, as awkward as frolicking cart horses. In this stage the insects are but short-lived, the males dying soon after the sexes pair, and the females living but a few days after they have laid their eggs in the ground.

The young grubs hatching among the roots of grass or grass-like plants commence to feed at once, and live in the earth in the larval stage for at least two years (so far as known), most of them changing to the dormant pupa from the middle of June to September of the second or third year after hatching, and becoming fully developed "June beetles" again, still in the earth, in August or in September of this same year. These beetles do not, as a rule, emerge from their earthen cells until the following spring, but spend the winter at rest, each in the underground cavity made originally by the grub while preparing to pupate. In May and June they come out and pair and lay their eggs as already related.

A single species (*Cyclocephala immaculata*) has a slightly different life history, the grub not pupating until spring. (Fig. 45–47.)

Our common and destructive white grubs all belong to the genera Lachnosterna and Cyclocephala, by far the greater number of species and individuals to the former genus, of which there are thirty-two species known to occur in Illinois. The genus Cyclocephala, on the other hand, contains but one species in this state. The life histories of these various kinds are not sufficiently different to make discrimination of species a matter of practical importance, and for economic purposes, consequently, the white grubs may usually be classed as one.

No wholly, or even fairly, satisfactory defence against them has yet been discovered, but in the contest with so abundant, so widespread, and so destructive an insect even imperfectly protective measures, or merely palliative ones, are worthy of the most careful attention. The practice of the farmers of the Old World, where a contest against closely related insects of like habit has been waged from time immemorial, is not usually applicable to American agriculture, but may nevertheless become so as conditions gradually change with the denser settlement of this country and a corresponding increase in the value of our agricultural products. I have consequently summarized the economic procedure of England, France, and Germany for the "cockchafer grub," the "*ver blanc*," and the "*engerling*,"—the names by which the European "white grubs" are known in those countries respectively.

INJURIES TO CORN AND OTHER VEGETATION.

The injuries of the American white grubs to corn may begin as soon as the roots of the young plant become large enough to attract the attention of a hungry insect, and may range —according to the age of the plant, the kind of weather, and the age and abundance of the grubs—all the way from a slight and temporary retardation of growth to an immediate and complete destruction of all the corn. An early loss of the tap-root exposes the plant to severe suffering by early drouth, and it is often so reduced in vigor from root injury that it fails to form brace roots at the proper time, and hence has so slight a hold upon the earth that it cannot keep itself erect or recover itself after prostration by a windy summer storm.

In any case where the plant is yellowed, or dwarfed, or killed outright,—especially if these appearances be most marked on the higher, lighter parts of the field,—the presence of white grubs may be suspected.

As the roots of an infested plant are evidently eaten away, injury by the white grub is not easily mistaken for any other, and the presence of the conspicuous insects themselves, in the earth among or beneath the roots, will commonly confirm the diagnosis. If they are not thus found where other evidence points to them as the cause of the injury, they may frequently be discovered by digging down a foot or two in the worst-injured tracts.

As a fair illustration of the extent and general effect of a severe attack on corn, our observations of their work in a twenty-acre field near Champaign, Illinois, are worthy of detailed report. This field of rich, black land had been heavily fertilized with straw-pile manure and seeded to timothy in 1884. It was pastured continuously until 1888, when it was left for hay, yielding a good crop of clean timothy that year. The sod was broken in the spring of 1889, and planted to corn May 10th, immediately after breaking. This first planting was taken by web worms and cutworms, but the second grew well, and promised an excellent crop until about tasseling time, when the owner noticed that much of the corn had a yellowish and unhealthy appearance, and that it blew down· readily when the ground was wet. These fallen hills pulled up easily, and the roots had a stubbed appearance, as if cut off near their origin. A search in the earth where the corn had stood commonly yielded six to twelve white grubs to a hill. The crop on two or three acres of the highest land was a total failure, and the yield was light on the lower ground.

The following year (1890) the field was plowed April 28th and planted again to corn, although an abundance of grubs were noticed when the plowing was done. Several hundred were, in fact, collected by us April 28th for breeding-cage experiments, nearly all belonging to the species *L. rugosa* (Fig. 42, 43, and 44). An estimate based·at this time on a count of the grubs found within the length of a rod.in a fourteen-inch furrow, gave between six and seven hundred to the square rod, or at the rate of two hundred and eighty-eight pounds per acre. By the time the young corn was six inches high about two-thirds of it had been destroyed by the grubs. The field was not replanted, but about the 10th of June it was twice harrowed and sown to hemp. On account of the lateness of the season and a midsummer drouth the hemp did not grow well, and about a hundred bushels of corn were finally taken from this twenty-acre field. July 26th, in the part of the field which had been worst infested, but three grubs and a single pupa were found in digging with a spade twenty holes, ranging in depth from a foot to twenty-six inches. On the 1st of September a trench four feet long, three feet wide, and two feet deep was dug in this same part with the result that only one adult June beetle and two long-dead larvæ were found. In another space eight feet long by three feet wide two adults and a single living larva were dug out, all the foregoing being within a foot of the surface. In two large areas turned over at the margin of the worst-infested spot, two living larvæ and one adult were taken, the former among the corn roots and the latter about ten inches down.

From these field observations, and parallel extensive breeding operations in the insectary, we have reason to infer the transformation to the imago stage during the season of 1890 of the greater part of the white grubs in this ground.

In 1891 the entire field was sown to hemp; but in 1892, three years after breaking, it was planted again to corn and again heavily injured by grubs. August 25th, a general survey of the field showed that no part was free from them, and that probably every acre had been injured more or less. The damage was most serious now on the lower ground, where a tract of about two acres bore only a few scattered stalks with ears. Most of the corn here had failed to tassel, and much of it had died when from eight or ten inches to about three feet high. Patches of a rod to two or three rods across on which the corn was dead or worthless were to be found in all parts of the field. Nearly all the foxtail-grass (*Setaria*) had also been killed, the roots being cut off just below the surface, and even the common purslane (*Portulaca*) was similarly destroyed. Most of the grubs were at this time within three inches of the surface, and were well scattered through the ground, being by no means confined to the hills of corn. In one selected area of four feet square, which included only two corn hills, eighty-one grubs were dug up, some scarcely beneath the surface, and none deeper than three inches. In another area of equal size, containing three corn hills, one hundred and thirty-six grubs were found, twenty-one of them in a single hill. Here, however, a few had burrowed to a depth of six inches. The grubs were at this time apparently from two-thirds to three-fourths grown, the most abundant species being *L. rugosa*—the same as that of the previous years.

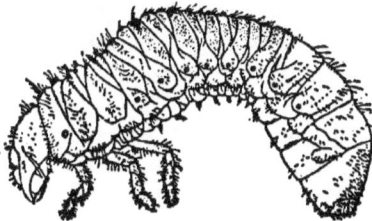

FIG. 42.—Grub of *Lachnosterna rugosa;* enlarged two and a half diameters.

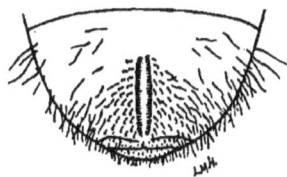

FIG. 43.—Last segment of grub, seen from beneath; enlarged six diameters.

In addition to affording an excellent illustration of the destructive capacity of the common white grubs, this record is of special interest as evidence that *L. rugosa* at least will lay its eggs and breed abundantly in fields of corn. On no other supposition can we explain the appearance of such vast numbers of partly grown larvæ three years after the ground was broken from grass in the spring; three years, that is, subsequent to the latest time at which the eggs could possibly have been laid in the grass. It seems very likely that this second lot of grubs was hatched from eggs laid in the corn in the summer of 1890 by the beetles which came out of the ground in this same field. If this inference be correct, it follows that planting to hemp for a year will not clear the ground of grubs.

A somewhat similar inference of a readiness to breed in corn is to be drawn from our observations on another plat of about four acres on the University farm near Urbana. This field, broken up in the spring of 1890 and put into corn, was planted in 1891 partly to corn, and partly to oats; in 1892 to oats and corn again, but with the areas reversed; and in 1893 to corn. On this the third year from sod, more than half the corn fell flat on the ground by the middle of September, most of the roots being eaten off by white grubs, of which three or four were commonly to be found in a hill. Owing to the consequent weakening of the plant the brace roots failed to form, the ears which set were small and very often imperfect, and a large percentage of the stalks were barren, the total height of the plant varying from six or eight feet to less than a foot. Even the tallest stalks were slender and unhealthy in appearance, the lower leaves, and sometimes practically the entire foliage of the plant, being as dry and brittle as in midwinter. Those stalks which had been killed early were usually so decayed as to be readily pulled apart at the nodes.

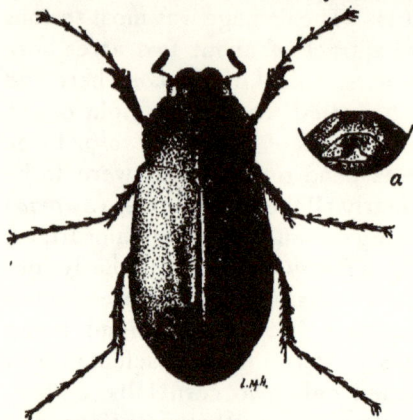

FIG. 44.—Beetle of *Lachnosterna rugosa*, male; enlarged two and a fifth diameters; *a*, last two ventral segments.

From these data we must conclude that the species concerned —which was either *inversa* or *fusca*—may live as a larva through four full years, making the entire life history cover a five-year period, or else that the eggs were laid later than 1889 in either corn or oats.

The white grubs taken by us in corn fields under circumstances to satisfy us that they either were or had been feeding on the roots of corn belong to eight species, as follows: *Lachnosterna fusca, tristis, inversa, hirticula, rugosa, gibbosa,* and *ilicis,* and *Cyclocephala immaculata.* Of these *L. fusca, inversa,* and *rugosa* are much the most common in such situations; and to them by far the greater part of the damage done to corn by the white grubs in central Illinois must be attributed.

Next to Indian corn, the crop most generally and seriously injured in Illinois by grubs is grass; and here the loss is the more serious because continuous and usually unnoticed. A very large number of these insects may live their long lives in the sod, feeding steadily at the roots, and thus diminishing the yield without actually deadening any continuous area. It is only when through uninterrupted multiplication they become excessively abundant, or when severe drouth checks the growth of vegetation, that brown patches may appear in midsummer, sometimes merging in areas of an acre or more over which the turf, loosened by a destruction of its roots, may be rolled up like a carpet.

That they were original inhabitants of the wild prairie sod is shown by the common testimony of old settlers, and by Walsh in the "Practical Entomologist" (Vol. I., p. 60), where he reports that in 1845 he found white grubs eating off young corn when it was a foot in height, in a field broken from prairie land the preceding year.

Patches of wheat, barley, and other small grains may be similarly killed, all underground parts of the plant being completely eaten up; but clover is scarcely ever damaged to any considerable degree, and grubs are relatively rare in clover sod mixed with grass. Their injuries to potatoes have often been reported, and are generally well known, and they are among the worst insect enemies of the strawberry grower. In regions where the sugar beet is an important crop, they are among the chief injurious insects to be taken into account. Young larches and evergreens are sometimes killed by them in the nursery rows, and probably every kind of delicately rooted shrub and of young fruit and forest tree is liable to destruction by them.

No general list of their food plants has ever been prepared, and nothing whatever is known of preferences with respect to food among the different species of grubs. That they may live for a considerable period on earth alone is shown by Dr. Riley, who says that he has known the larvæ of the common May beetle to feed for three months on nothing but pure soil;* and Professor

---

*St. Louis "Globe-Democrat," March 25, 1876.

Perkins, of Vermont, has kept individuals of all ages alive for weeks, and sometimes for months, in sand more free from organic matter than the soil of any field fit for growing crops.* The remarkable fact that the grubs may eat locusts' eggs in the ground has been mentioned in the First Report of the U. S. Entomological Commission (p. 305).

The beetles of the white grub feed most frequently on the leaves of various species of trees. Oak, hickory, ash, box elder, elm, chestnut, butternut, black walnut, basswood, hackberry, hazel, willow, black locust, mountain ash, tame and wild cherry, and pear are the species positively known by us, by personal observation, to be eaten by the adult beetles of various species; and apple, plum, Lombardy poplar, sweet gum (Liquidambar), maple, and birch may be added to the list on other authority. When a tree is much infested, the leaves are eaten entire except perhaps a stub of the petiole, or the petiole and a part of the midrib. Even the bark of the younger twigs may be gnawed away. Two species, *hirticula* and *fusca*, have been charged with an almost wanton injury to the foliage of trees (oak and chestnut) done by gnawing through the leaf petioles without eating the leaves (Proc. Ent. Soc. Washington, Vol. II., p. 59), and we have noted the same habit as occasionally exhibited to some small extent in the "artificial forest" on the University premises at Urbana. The imagos sometimes eat the leaves of blue-grass also, and we have once found them feeding on heads of clover and once on corn. Several species have been known to eat the leaves of raspberries ("Insect Life," Vol. I., p. 366).

These notes on the food of the beetles are of interest because of the damage sometimes done by these insects, especially to trees on lawns, during the brief period of their excessive abundance in May and June, but still more because it is in the adult stage that the white grubs are most susceptible to organized attack. If they are ever thoroughly mastered by the farmers of America, it will apparently be by concerted measures, possibly supplemented by legal requirement, for the destruction of June beetles before they have laid their eggs.

LIFE HISTORY AND HABITS.

The adult beetles of the more abundant genus Lachnosterna, hibernating in the earth in the cells where they originated, emerge in spring and early summer at periods varying according to the species of beetle, the general advancement of the season, and the character of the weather at the time. Warm and genial days in

*Fifth Ann. Rep. Vt. Agr. Exper. Station (1891), p. 151.

spring often bring them suddenly out in myriads where previously only scattered individuals have been seen, and their flight at night is of course more free when the weather is warm than when their energies are chilled by cold and storms.

As a rule, the males are not only the first to appear, but surpass the females in number, taking the season through. They also come to lights much more freely than the females, as is shown by a comparison of our collections made at lights with those made the same night from trees on which the beetles were feeding. The 7th of May, 1891, for example, a collection of *L. inversa* made with a lantern trap contained 1,210 males and twenty-four females, —a ratio of fifty to one,—while we took from trees the same night one hundred and twenty-two males and seventy-three females— less than two to one. Taking all our collections of this species for the summer of 1891, we find that in those from lights (1,418 specimens) the males are to the females as fifty-one to one, while in those from trees (271 specimens) the ratio was one and one-half to one. This is, however, much greater than the usual difference in other Lachnosternas, the species evidently varying with reference to their sensibility to light.

However taken and at whatever part of the season, it is rarely that the females exceed or even equal the males in the same collection. Throwing together 2,600 specimens of several species, taken at frequent intervals throughout the season of 1891, the sexes of which we have separated, it appears that the ratio of males to females at lights was 16.5 to 1, and from trees and various surface shelters (839 specimens) 1.3 to 1. My data on this subject may be conveniently exhibited in the following tabular form :

Species.	Dates.	At Light.		On Trees, etc.	
		No. of specimens.	Ratio of male to female.	No. of specimens.	Ratio of male to female.
Fusca	April 18—June 4..	94	2.2	193	1.3
Hirticula	April 29—June 24..	185	4.6	352	1.3
Inversa	April 29—June 28..	1,418	51.0	271	1.5
Tristis...............	May 7	135	1.4	—	—
Gibbosa.............	May 15—June 24..	42	13.0	20	2.3

The adult beetles emerging from the ground, flying about at night * in search of food, pair in the trees, to which they resort in myriads, and retreat again to the earth by day. Their first flight is made in the early evening, beginning at dusk, as they pass from

* A single species has been observed to fly by day in Utah. (Proc. Ent. Soc. Washington, Vol. II., p. 241.)

the ground where they have lain hidden by day to the trees on which they feed. With the advent of day they fly from the trees to the earth, and hide themselves an inch or less underground, or sometimes merely creep under fallen grass and other similar shelter.

Particulars concerning this retreat to their hiding places at the dawn of day are given in notes made by Mr. John Marten and Mr. Philip Hucke, detailed for night-work on June beetles May 19, 1891.

3:45 a. m. Mr. Hucke reports the occasional dropping of a beetle from trees in the artificial forest (chiefly butternuts and hickories) where these observations were made. At 4:05, an occasional beetle still dropping to the ground without making any effort to fly. At 4:10 the air suddenly became full of flying beetles. One and then another began to make a buzzing noise with its wings, when, as if at a general signal, they deserted the trees in thousands, and by 4:25 everything was still again and nearly every one was gone.

Within the woods the beetles flew to a distance from the trees about equal to the height from which they started, the lower ones on the trees making a somewhat longer flight proportionally. Striking against the weeds and undergrowth, they folded their wings, and by 4:30 o'clock reached the ground within a hundred feet of the trees from which they took their flight. Probably in a clearer place they would make longer flights.

The Egg.— Some of the species begin to lay their eggs in the earth early in June, and this operation is in progress for about a month. The eggs are placed from an inch to three inches beneath the surface, each enclosed separately in a cavity just large enough to hold it, several, however, being frequently placed near each other, but never, according to our observations, in a common cell. There appears in no case any special preparation of the soil or chamber containing the egg, the statement commonly made to the effect that the eggs are laid in a ball of earth being clearly erroneous. The eggs are oblong-oval when first deposited, but soon swell by absorption to a nearly spherical form. The males begin to die not long after pairing, and the females also perish as their ovaries are spent. The eggs hatch in from ten to eighteen days, according to our experiments. As the data upon which these statements are based are few, they may profitably be given in some detail.

Larval Period.—Our knowledge of the length of life of the white grubs in the larval stage is based solely upon inferences mostly drawn from the varying sizes of the grubs that appear in collections made at any given time. Since the eggs are all deposited practically within a month, and since the larva grows but slowly, differences in size due to variations in time of hatching must be but small. It is easily seen, however, from almost any large collection made in spring or early summer at one time and place that grubs of the same species or group can be readily assorted into two lots differing notably in size, and never, so far as my observation goes, into more than two.* This is readily to be explained on the supposition that the larger specimens are two years old that season and that the smaller have hatched from eggs laid the preceding summer. Upon this supposition the Lachnosterna larva lives as a grub a trifle over two full years, changes to the pupa and imago at the beginning of the third year of its life, and emerges from the earth an adult, prepared to lay its eggs, at the end of this three-year period.

The growing grubs feed, of course, only during the season of growing vegetation, usually retiring from the middle to the last of November to a depth beneath the surface varying according to the severity of the winter weather, and coming up again within reach of food commonly some time in March or early April.

The time and place of hibernation have their especial economic interest, since while in their usual winter quarters the white grubs are far beyond the reach of any agricultural operations. The distance to which they retreat in this latitude is about a foot and a half, if I may judge from a single observation made November 29, 1886, in a badly infested field of wheat in Sangamon county, Illinois. Here, around the margins of denuded patches,—the ground being frozen some four inches deep,—the white grubs were found repeatedly in numbers averaging four or five to the square foot at a depth varying from a foot and a half to two feet. In 1890 they had already come up, in the pastures, from their winter quarters by the 24th of March; were still at the surface in their usual number during the latter part of October; and had not wholly withdrawn by November 25th—although at this last date most had gone beyond the reach of the plow. Notwithstanding this well-marked habit of retreat at the approach of winter, they occasionally linger at the surface and hibernate at a depth scarcely greater than that at which they are to be found during the summer season.

Pupation and Formation of the Beetle.—The full-grown white grubs, presumed to be two years old according to the preceding section, will live an active life in the earth, feeding freely from

---

* To verify this statement it is necessary that the observer should learn to distinguish species or at least groups of species of these insects in the grub and larval stage.

March to June or July, during which months they change to the pupa a few inches under ground, in oval cells made by the grub by turning about in the earth. In this smooth-walled chamber the cuticular remnant of the last moult will be found enclosed with the pupa—that is, the crust of the head of the grub and shriveled fragments of its last skin. Our first date for this pupal transformation of *L. inversa* is June 13, 1889, but Professor Perkins notes the pupation of two larvæ out of several hundred early in May. In this chamber they lie until August or September, when they change to the June beetle, *fusca* and *gibbosa* as early as August 11th, and others—at least individuals of *implicita*, for example— not before September 17th. A small percentage of the adults thus formed late in the summer and in early fall, may escape from the earth before the winter opens, but this is relatively a rare occurrence, the great mass of the generation continuing through the winter in the pupal cells within which they originated. They are to be found in winter from no more than two or three inches to about ten inches beneath the surface. Hence they escape in spring, as already described, pairing and laying their eggs for the generation following.

From the foregoing it will be seen that the white grubs of the genus Lachnosterna hibernate in two stages only, those of larva and imago, the grubs themselves representing at least two generations.

Cyclocephala. (Fig. 45–47.)—The white grubs of the genus Cyclocephala differ from those of the various species of Lachnosterna in so far, at least, as to hibernate in the larval stage, to pupate in May and June, and to emerge as beetles in June and July —later on an average than the species of the other genus. Pupation is consequently earlier than in Lachnosterna, and the emergence of the imago occurs later in the season, the essential difference being that adults of Cyclocephala escape from the earth one or two months after the completion of their larval life, while those of Lachnosterna continue in the earthen cells as pupæ and imagos about ten months. The difference in the economic application of these biographies is not, however, very great, since the period of active larval life of Cyclocephala seems to terminate on an average only three or four weeks before that of Lachnosterna. My detailed notes on the transformation of white grubs belonging to this genus are but few in number, but as they accord with those already given by entomologists, they serve to support the common statements concerning the life history of these beetles.

Our only species in Illinois is *C. immaculata*, and its larvæ occur in grass with the other white grubs, and have been found infesting corn on sod.

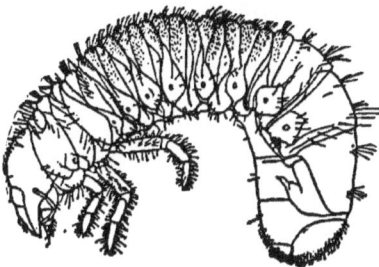

FIG. 45.—Grub of *Cyclocephala immaculata;* enlarged three and a third diameters.

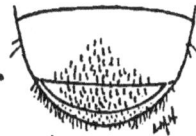

FIG. 46.—Last segment of grub, seen from beneath; enlarged six diameters.

NATURAL ENEMIES.

In the struggle for existence the white grubs and the June beetles enjoy many pronounced advantages, and are subject to relatively few and feeble checks on their multiplication. The large size and the subterranean habit of the grubs protect them in great

FIG. 47.—Beetle of *Cyclocephala immaculata;* enlarged three diameters.

measure against two of the three principal classes of natural enemies of insect larvæ; namely, birds and insect parasites. They are more liable to fungus parasitism, it is true, but many kinds of much less abundant insects suffer far more heavily therefrom, and authentic reports of the notable destruction of our American white grubs by fungus parasites are rare. The beetles are especially protected by their large size and heavy armor, by their nocturnal habit and their skill in hiding themselves by day, by the enormous numbers in which they appear, and by the relatively short term of their adult life. Cold and heat, drouth and wet weather have little noticeable effect upon these insects in any stage, and even starvation does not kill the grubs, for in the absence of other food they can live for months on earth alone.

Great as the number doubtless is of individuals of the several species which fall victims during the year to various enemies and other hostile agencies, the evidence now before us does not warrant us in placing any considerable reliance on these natural checks to the multiplication of the white grubs, but we are rather led to conclude that American agriculture must look to its own resources for a remedy. If, however, we take into account the fact that our common white grubs are native insects, most of them living originally in the prairie sod, which formed a denser, more uniform, and more continuous covering to the surface of the country than the crops now raised by the farmer, and further recall the fact that under these primitive conditions these insects rarely produced any conspicuous effect upon our native vegetation, we may infer with some confidence that they are not likely to increase indefinitely and inordinately, but that the natural checks which held them primitively within a certain well-defined limit will reassert themselves under the not very different conditions of a developed agriculture. Such data as we have concerning the enemies of these insects, animal and vegetable, are presented here more as an indication of the incompleteness of our knowledge, than because of their present practical value.

Birds.—White grubs and June beetles are eaten to some extent by a considerable variety of birds, doubtless by many more than my cullings of the scanty literature of this subject have brought to light.

In my own studies, I have found June beetles eaten by the robin, catbird, brown thrush, wood thrush, hermit thrush, bluebird, and meadow lark; Mr. E. V. Wilcox has found both June beetles and white grubs in the stomachs of robins; and Glover long ago recorded the occurrence of June beetles in the stomach of a woodpecker (Rep. U. S. Comm. Agr. 1865, p. 38). Dr. A. K. Fisher reports the occurrence of these beetles in the food of the red-tailed hawk, the red-shouldered hawk, the broad-winged hawk, the sparrow hawk, the screech owl, and the great horned owl; and white grubs in that of the red-shouldered hawk, the sparrow hawk, and the barred owl. Dr. C. V. Riley's assistants recognized fragments of the beetles in the stomachs of six English sparrows, and four large white grubs in one of this species, out of five hundred and twenty-two specimens examined.

To this list I can add only the crow and the blue jay, on the authority of Dr. B. H. Warren, author of the " Birds of Pennsylvania," the chuck-will's widow ("Insect Life," Vol. II., p. 189), the king-bird (Lintner), and the crow blackbird, whose habit of picking up white grubs after the plow is a matter of common observation.

Of these twenty species, taking into account their numbers and their feeding habits, I judge that the robin, the catbird, the brown thrush, and the crow blackbird devour much the largest numbers of these insects,* although it is possible that if the

---

* Nine out of forty-four robins shot by me in April, May, and June had eaten June beetles; six catbirds out of forty-one; and twelve brown thrushes out of forty-three.

smaller insectivorous hawks—the sparrow hawk especially—were permitted to increase freely they would equal or surpass any of these, because of the greater number of insects which they take at a meal.   Chickens, ducks, and turkeys are fond of white grubs, and may often be seen scattered over freshly plowed ground in search of them and other subterranean insects.

Mammals.—The only native mammals known to feed on these insects in any considerable numbers are moles, ground squirrels, and skunks—none of them very likely to be tolerated by the farmer, whatever may be their insectivorous habits.

Among the domestic animals, pigs are well known as eager hunters for white grubs, in search of which they dilligently root up an infested turf; a fact which may sometimes be advantageously applied for the protection of corn to follow upon grass.

Insects.—The special insect enemies of the white grubs now on record belong to three or, possibly, four species, two of them hymenopterous and one dipterous, a second dipterous insect bred by us from dead white grubs being doubtfully parasitic.   To this number I am able to add another hymenopterous parasite, *Pelecinus polyturator*, a remarkable insect whose larval history has heretofore been wholly unknown.   From a collection of white grubs obtained from an orchard at Champaign, Illinois, May 9, 1892, and kept in a breeding cage at my office insectary, a specimen of *Pelecinus polyturator* emerged August 26, 1892.   As the parasite was seen in the act of emerging from its pupal envelope, there can be no doubt of either the fact or the date.   An examination of the remains of the grub containing the pupa skin of the parasite showed that the former belonged to the species *L. gibbosa*.   My office specimens of the adult of this parasite are recorded under nine collection numbers, all bearing dates in late summer and early fall—July 21st, 26th, August 1st, 2d, 11th, 16th, 28th, and September 1st and 16th.   It is hence probably single brooded, maturing in July and August.

Perhaps the most destructive insect enemy of the white grub is *Tiphia inornata*, Say, a hymenopterous species which we have never bred, but which has been reported by Dr. Riley to occur occasionally in very large numbers in ground infested by Lachnosterna larvæ.   He says: "One can scarcely dig for half an hour in any soil in this part of the country, without meeting with a curious egg-shaped cocoon, of a pale golden brown or buff color, and with a soft exterior surface, in touch as well as in color reminding one of the punk used by dentists.   Upon cutting this cocoon open, it will be found to consist of about a dozen delicate layers, the outer ones soft and loosely spun, the inner ones more and more compact and paler in color. Within this cocoon, if fresh, there will be found a whitish grub which, though lacking legs, has the joints of the body, at the sides, swollen so as to look like the fleshy pseudopods possessed by many larvæ. * * * From having repeatedly found the head parts of some Lamellicorn larva attached to these cocoons, I had long suspected that such larvæ formed the food of this Tiphia, and on carefully examining these head-parts I recognized them as belonging to the common white grub. But all doubt as to this fly's being parasitic on said white grub ceased when, in 1872, Mr. A. W. Smith, of St. Louis, brought me a number of the cocoons which he had taken from a low part of his farm on the Illinois bottom, where the white grub was very thick, and the yellow cocoons so numerous as to attract attention."

Ophion bifoveolatum is likewise reported by Riley as a white grub parasite (Proc. Ent. Soc. Washington, Vol. II., p. 134), and this was quite probably the species of Ophion bred at my office in 1886. From white grubs brought to the insectary April 27th the specimen emerged May 11th, but was lost from my collections before being determined specifically.

A tachinid fly has also been found parasitic on the grubs (Proc. Ent. Soc. Washington, Vol. II., p. 134), and a second fly, *Microphthalma nigra*, Macq., has been repeatedly bred by us from the dead bodies of white grubs. The habits of the family Dexidæ, to which this last mentioned insect belongs, make it doubtful, however, if these flies may not have developed from eggs laid on the bodies of grubs already dead.

Tiphia inornata, mentioned above, ought probably to be called a predaceous rather than a parasitic insect, as it attacks the grub from without, and devours it bodily. Ants destroy white grubs in breeding-cages, and very possibly attack them sometimes in the field. It is quite likely that various other predaceous insect species, ground beetles especially, may devour white grubs occasionally, as has indeed been suggested by Riley (Sixth Ent. Rep. Mo.), but I have no record of precise observations to that effect. The fact that the beetles may sometimes fall a prey to carnivorous insects, is shown by two specimens brought to my office by a student of the University, May 21, 1891. One of these was an example of *L. hirticula*, which he had found with the tip of its abdomen torn open, crawling up a stem of grass. The other was a *Chlænius tomentosus*, found clinging to the Lachnosterna and feeding upon its viscera, partly drawn out of the wound. The frequency with which mites are found clustered upon white grubs in their earthen cells, especially upon those recently dead or in a weakened condition, has given rise to the supposition, hitherto not experimentally verified, that these mites may be parasitic on the grubs.

On the whole, the general tenor of our own observations, as well as those published by other entomologists, must lead us to attach comparatively little economic importance to the insect enemies of white grubs, whether predaceous or parasitic.

Reptiles and Amphibians.—The fact that the toad occasionally eats June beetles has been reported (Proc. Ent. Soc. Washington, Vol. I., p. 69), and could no doubt be verified extensively by dissections of toads made at times when the June beetle is abroad. Frogs must likewise be placed on the list of the natural enemies of these beetles. Prof. Perkins, of the University of Vermont, has found as many as ten in the stomach of a single frog of medium size. It is altogether likely that insectivorous reptiles, serpents especially, would be found to destroy a still greater number of these insects, but no studies have been made, to my knowledge, on this point.

Fungi.—But one contagious disease of the American white grub occurring in nature has been positively and definitely connected with a fungus parasite. This parasite (*Cordyceps melolonthæ*) has been several times referred to in economic literature, first in the "American Journal of Science and Arts" (August, 1824). It was treated at length in an illustrated article published by Riley in the "American Entomologist" for June, 1880. According to a correspondent of Walsh's in 1869, it has sometimes been very common in Virginia; and Mrs. Treat reported the occurrence of thousands of infested specimens in Benton county, Iowa, in 1865. Perkins mentions it as infesting grubs of Lachnosterna in Vermont. This species is, so far as known, incapable of artificial cultivation, and could consequently be used for insecticide purposes only by distributing as carriers of infection white grubs which had been in contact with others infested with it. Indications have not been wanting of the occurrence of a bacterial disease native to our Lachnosterna larvæ, but no precise studies have been made sufficient to warrant the assertion that such bacterial diseases really occur. The common insect parasite, *Sporotrichum globuliferum*, the so-called white fungus of the chinch bug, has never been found by us infesting Lachnosterna larvæ in a state of nature, although these larvæ have been proven quite susceptible to it in the course of our experimental work. June beetles have been frequently found, however, with this fungus growing upon their dead bodies, but, for all that is clearly known to the contrary, it may have taken its start upon them after the death of the beetles.

In Europe, according to Giard and Krassilstschik, three diseases of the European white grubs have been detected: one of them due to a fungous infection by the species most commonly known as *Isaria densa*, Link, (=*Botrytis tenella*, Saccardo); and the other two, bacterial diseases studied by the last named author.

PREVENTIVE AND REMEDIAL MEASURES.

If we use the word remedy for measures intended to arrest an injury already begun, and prevention for measures applied in advance of such injury, we must say that efficient remedies for the injuries of white grubs are but little applicable to their work in corn, and that we are confined consequently, for the main purposes of this article, to a discussion of preventive measures only. Such measures of prevention may be either local or general: applied, in the first case, to the field in which corn is to be planted, and intended to forestall injury in that field only; or, in the second case, applied elsewhere or more comprehensively, with a view to a more general effect in reducing the number of white grubs over a larger area.

Local preventive measures can take effect only on the white grubs themselves, while the most valuable general measures are those directed to the destruction of the June beetles before their eggs are laid.

Local Prevention.—It is now well settled, as has been shown in the preceding pages, that at least some species of the white grubs may be freely and abundantly bred in fields of corn; but it still remains true that by far the greater number of those in the country at any time have arisen from eggs laid by the beetles in ground bearing a crop of grass; and that corn is consequently much more likely to be damaged if planted on sod than if it follows clover, some small grain, or corn itself. The first effort of the corn farmer threatened by these insects should consequently be directed to clearing the grubs out of the grass land which he wishes to plant to corn. For this purpose it is very desirable that hogs should be pastured for a considerable time on meadows or pastures before plowing for corn, and that they should also be given the run of the field while it is being plowed. This measure will be practically useless, however, under ordinary circumstances, if resorted to later than October or earlier than April, as in the interval between these months the grubs will be beyond the reach of pigs, buried in their winter quarters.

Further, I do not, myself, in the least doubt the great profit to the average farmer of providing for the collection of white grubs after the plow, by hand, in soil where they are particularly abundant, especially where any kind of cheap labor may be had. In estimating the value of this method, we should bear in mind the fact that a small number of grubs may do a great amount of harm to young corn on comparatively clean ground, because of the small amount of vegetation offered to them as food while the corn is young.

Next, we should take into account the relatively small damage done to clover by the grubs, and the further fact that we have no present evidence that the eggs of the June beetle are ever laid in clover land. It is consequently a good practice, so far as grub injury is concerned, to insert clover (sown perhaps with oats) between grass and corn in the rotation ; and this is especially to be advised on light soils, not perfectly adapted to corn. Here it will have the effect not only to eliminate the grubs in part, but also to diminish the damage to the following crops of corn by increasing the strength of the land, thus helping the corn plant to withstand such loss of roots as it may nevertheless be subjected to. In this connection it need hardly be said that a generous treatment of the soil by heavy fertilization, thorough cultivation, and the like, will diminish loss to corn by enabling plants attacked to throw out new roots more vigorously to take the place of those eaten by the grubs. Indeed, by some most intelligent and successful farmers, high fertilizing with frequent rotation is regarded as the essential and sufficient defense against these insects.

The management of corn on lands containing grubs should also be directed especially to the protection of the plant from drouth, as, in the presence of these insects, dry weather takes a double effect by retarding root growth under circumstances which require it to be vigorously stimulated instead.

To prevent the laying of the eggs of the June beetle in the *corn field* in May or June, it is desirable that the ground should be kept practically free from weeds at that time, as it is well known that a surface growth of vegetation is a strong attraction to these insects searching for places suitable for the support of the young. Some of our more recent observations show that the beetles are likely to deposit their eggs in the field from which they themselves have emerged, provided that it offers them suitable conditions—a fact which makes it clearly inadvisable that a field which is badly infested one year, should be planted to corn the next.

General Prevention.—The principal and most effective preventive measures of general promise are those for the collection and destruction of the June beetles before they have laid their eggs. They are practically confined to the following four methods, mentioned in the order of their importance : (a) shaking and jarring down the beetles at night from the trees in which they feed, and their collection on sheets or cloth-covered frames similar to those in use for the peach and plum curculio; (b) exposing light traps early in the evening in places frequented by the beetles; (c) the spraying of trees to which they resort, with Paris green or other suitable insecticide; and (d) the turning of pigs into woodlands, forest plantations, and the like, where the June beetles conceal themselves by day.

These are all measures calling for coöperative action by all, or at least the greater part, of the farmers of a neighborhood, since it is useless to expect any pronounced effect from isolated and individual action. They can only be carried out by previous agreement of those interested, by the offer of premiums for the beetles, or by the passage and enforcement of laws bearing equally upon all. In estimating the value of these methods it should be remembered that each female beetle is the average equivalent of a large number of grubs.

In illustration of the effectiveness of the first mentioned of these methods, I quote from notes of Assistants Marten and Hucke, made in 1891.

May 19th, 2:40 a. m. Shaking the trees in the University forest plantation made the beetles fall very easily, the second shake generally getting all, or nearly all, there were in a tree. Those shaken from the trees made no effort to fly up again, and only one such came to the lantern trap near by.

3:45 a. m. The beetles apparently as abundant as ever on butternut and hickory. The lightest shake of either of these trees brings down the beetles by dozens. Butternut trees six to eight inches in diameter drop them in considerable numbers when shaken by the hands—so easily are they detached.

From other notes it is apparent that the June beetles cling more closely to the trees early in the evening,—from eight to ten o'clock,—a fact doubtless to be connected with the gradually stupefying effect of the night dews and the cooler air towards morning.

This is the standard method in both France and Germany for the control of injuries by the European white grubs. The results attained in the former country are shown by an article, "La Chasse aux Hannetons," published in the *Revue de deux Mondes* for 1878. In consequence of an offer of premiums for beetles in the department of *Seine-Inférieure*, 1,149,000,000 of these cockchafers were collected and paid for in that year, at an expenditure of $16,000. It was estimated that these beetles would have given origin the following year to 23,000,000,000 white grubs. The proprietor of an establishment for the manufacture of sugar from beets, whose crop was seriously affected by the ravages of the grubs, offered a prize of $4 for each one hundred kilogrammes (about two hundred and twenty pounds avoirdupois) of the beetles, and obtained as a consequence 28,000,000 cockchafers—equivalent to 560,000,000 grubs the following year.

Details of the common procedure in France are given by A. Wallés in "Bulletin de la Société Centrale d'Apiculture et d'Insectologie" for June, 1890. "It would be a mistake," he says, "to wait until the cockchafers [English name for the European equivalent of our June beetles] have emerged, since the whole benefit of the capture of the beetles will be lost if the females are given time to lay their eggs. Measures for the destruction of these insects must be taken, consequently, from the time that a few begin to appear. Further, if in certain parts of the territory involved the capture of the beetles is neglected, the good effect of the procedure will be considerably diminished. These two points are essential and imperative.

"The cockchafer catchers should be provided with hooked poles, with an awning cloth, or the like, and with bags for their catch. It will be well for them to go in little groups, and to make their rounds from the time of the first appearance of the insect. This last observation is most important. On the 12th of May, for example [in France], no more than twenty per cent. of the cockchafers captured in the trees will be females. A little later, on the contrary, the males will have disappeared, and scarcely any but females will be found. These, however, will have laid their eggs.

"The beetles may be most easily shaken down from the trees in which they are concealed, at the dawn of day, when they are still stupid with the coolness of the night, and this is, consequently, the time at which these collections should be made. Two persons will do well to work together when tall trees are to be visited. One strikes the branches and shakes them by means of the hook fastened into the end of his pole, while the other picks up the beetles. They can, of course, change places occasionally. When there is grass under the trees a cloth must be spread to catch the beetles, which would otherwise often be lost. It will be very easy to clear trees of smaller size by shaking them energetically, but not violently enough to break them.

"It is perhaps in the canton of Mayenne that the cockchafer hunt is pursued by the inhabitants with the greatest method, energy, and perseverance. There those engaged in the chase of the beetles are divided into squads of four (men, women, or children), each of which is furnished with the following instruments: (1) A sheet of burlap three yards by two, in the ends of which two flexible sticks are fastened. Strings intended to support the apparatus are attached to these sticks. (2) A long pole armed with an iron hook. (3) A sack of coarse cloth. The squad being thus equipped, two hold the sheet extended under the branches. Owing to the flexibility of the rods at the end, the surface of the sheet easily takes the concave form of a common hammock. The branches are then shaken with the hand or with the hooked stick, and the cockchafers fall upon the cloth and accumulate in the center."

Between 2 and 5 o'clock a. m. is the best time for capturing our American June beetles. If they are thus collected in very great numbers, they may be most conveniently killed by throwing them into tubs or barrels of water with kerosene on the surface. If the number is so great as to be likely to be offensive if left to decay, they may be scattered upon the fields as a fertilizer.

The foregoing method is but little likely to be brought into use on the scale required to make it effective unless the white grubs become, at least locally, more destructive than they are at present in any part of the State of Illinois. It is quite within the bounds of possibility, however, that this or some similar method will be ultimately forced upon the American farmer.

Our June beetles are strongly attracted by lights; a disposition which may be used for their destruction in fields. An apparatus consisting of a lantern suspended over a tub of water, placed in or near trees or groves resorted to by the beetles, will often collect large numbers of the adult insects, which, flying against the lantern, drop into the water, where they are readily killed if a little kerosene has been poured over the surface. This method is, however, of little value as compared with that above described, since it attracts males in very much greater proportion than females—sometimes fifty of the former to one of the latter. It is also ineffective on moonlight nights, and when the weather is cool or windy; is much more expensive; and, under the most favorable circumstances, less thoroughgoing. Its effect is shown by office notes made in 1888 and 1891. June 9th of the former year one hundred and twenty-seven beetles were caught in a pan fifteen inches across partly filled with water and kerosene, above which an ordinary lantern was suspended, the apparatus being placed on a bench under trees, in Urbana, Ill. A similar experiment, made May 7, 1891, with a tub of water and oil and a common kerosene lamp yielded 1,290 beetles, of which all but forty-one were males. In this case the trap was placed in a small forest plantation on the University farm in Urbana. These beetles were all taken between 7:45 and 9:15 p. m., after which only now and then one would come to the light. Later in the season no doubt the proportion of females to males would have been greater; but statements made in another part of this article, under the head "Life History and Habits," show that the disproportion continues throughout the season.

The spraying of trees most resorted to for food is a possible measure, since the beetles are killed by arsenical poisons—a fact demonstrated by laboratory experiments made by us in 1888 with oak leaves dipped in Paris green mixture, one ounce to twenty gallons of water. The expense of a general application of such an insecticide will, however, prevent its common use.

When pigs can be turned, in May and June, into groves, orchards, or forests infested by the beetles, they cannot fail to destroy immense numbers of them, since they eat them eagerly, and can easily find them, hidden as they commonly are by day barely under the surface of the ground. This is a measure only occasionally applicable.

Remedial Measures.—Direct remedies for the attacks of white grubs are either inapplicable to the corn field, are of doubtful economic value, or are too little understood, as yet, to make them worthy of recommendation. For example, kerosene emulsion may properly be applied to infested lawns, and, if followed by a copious watering, may kill large numbers of the grubs, but the cost of this material and treatment will preclude its use against grubs in corn; and kainit and other potash fertilizers (the sulphate especially) will destroy grubs in the earth, but for this purpose must be used at a rate inadmissible in farm practice—more than a ton per acre according to Prof. Perkins (Fifth Ann. Rep. Vt. Agr. Exper. Station, p. 152).

Among remedial measures of uncertain value may be mentioned the cultivation and dissemination of the fungus parasites of the white grub—uncertain because not yet thoroughly tested, and because such tests as have been made do not demonstrate the practical utility of the method.

These parasitic fungi do, however, sometimes spontaneously destroy immense numbers of white grubs in the field, and some of them can be easily cultivated in quantity outside the body of the insect—almost as easily as mushrooms may be grown for the market. The subject of the fungous diseases of these insects is therefore a very suitable one for investigation, and should undoubtedly be most thoroughly studied from every point of view.

THE GREEN JUNE BEETLE.

(*Allorhina nitida*, L.)

FIG. 48.—Green June Beetle: *a*, larva; *b*, pupa; *c*, male beetle;—all enlarged 1½ diameters; *d, e, f, g,* mandible, antenna, leg, and maxilla of larva,—more enlarged.

The larva of the green June beetle, *Allorhina nitida*, commonly known as a white grub where it occurs, is distinguishable from the species of Lachnosterna and Cyclocephala by its somewhat larger size when full grown; by the thick covering of short stiff hairs easily visible to the naked eye; but especially by the difference in its method of locomotion upon a hard surface. The common white grubs (Lachnosterna) creep only by means of their legs, dragging the heavy abdomen clumsily along; but the larva of the green June beetle, when thrown upon a hard surface, turns immediately upon its back, and moves somewhat easily in this position by alternate contraction and expansion of the segments of the body, using the stiff hairs upon the back as an aid.

This is a southern species, and in the Southern States largely replaces Lachnosterna, its larva being there known as *the* white grub. In Central Illinois it occurs but rarely, but becomes noticeably abundant in the southern part of the State, where it has been occasionally reported as injurious in a small way. Although it has not been found in corn fields, its food and habits are such as to make it altogether likely that under favoring circumstances it might injure corn in the same manner as the Lachnosterna larva— or rather as the larva of Cyclocephala, which it more closely resembles in its life history. The grub is normally a grass insect, but infests likewise strawberry fields, and has been found by Dr. Riley to feed in confinement upon the roots of wheat. It seems to be less dependent upon living vegetation than even the white grubs, apparently living much more generally upon a rich soil. Indeed, the beetles seem to be attracted to manured land when about to lay their eggs, or to that which has been heavily mulched or contains an unusual amount of decomposing vegetation. Townsend has found them living in clean earth under circumstances to indicate a carnivorous habit.

The life history of this insect is, as already intimated, different from that of Lachnosterna, especially in the fact that pupation of the larva takes place in May, the beetles issuing in June. Its length of larval life is not known, nor the precise time or place of oviposition.

PRIONUS GRUBS.

FIG. 49.—Prionus grub; natural size.

The occasional occurrence in corn of large thick-bodied grubs belonging to a different family from the common white grubs of this article, calls merely for general mention. These are the larvæ of two species of large brown, flattish, long-horned beetles, and belong to the genus Prionus (*P. imbricornis* and *P. laticollis*). They are sometimes common in prairie or pasture sod, where they feed upon the roots of grass, and have also been a few times reported in corn fields in Illinois and Missouri, doing an injury apparently identical with that of the white grubs. These grubs are at once distinguishable from the latter insects by their greater size (3 mm. in length and nearly half as thick when full grown), by the form of the body (tapering from the head backwards), and by the fact that it is little, if at all, curved. They are, further, at once distinguishable by the rudimentary and inconspicuous character of their legs. They are much more generally known to economic entomology for their injuries to the roots of the vine and apple and some forest trees than for their agricultural relations.

FIG. 50.—Pupa of Prionus; natural size.

FIG. 51.—Beetle of *Prionus laticollis;* natural size.

b. *Roots penetrated, perforated, irregularly burrowed, and more
or less eaten off and eaten up. Underground parts of stalk
usually also similarly injured.*
Wireworms in soil among the roots.

(For a discussion of the wireworm injury to ·corn, see this
report, p. 224.)

*Small, slender, soft-bodied, white or yellowish-white grubs in the
roots and earth.*

The Southern Corn Root Worm.

(*Diabrotica 12-punctata*, Oliv.)

(Fig. 52–56.)

Injuries to corn by the southern corn root worm have **not**
been seen by us in Northern Illinois and but rarely in the central
part of the State, but they are more likely to occur southward.
Outside this State they have been recognized by entomologists in
Ohio, Indiana, Kentucky, Arkansas, Mississippi, Louisiana, Alabama, South Carolina, Virginia, and Maryland. As the beetle
occurs from Canada southward through the Atlantic region, and
thence to Minnesota, Kansas, Louisiana, and Mexico, it will probably be found much more generally present in corn fields than the
above report would indicate.

Its injuries are very similar in general character and effect to
those of the much more abundant and better known northern corn
root worm (*Diabrotica longicornis*), with which they have doubtless
frequently been confounded. They are distinguishable with some
difficulty from those due to the various species of wireworms, and
it will often require the recognition of the larva itself to determine
positively to which of these two classes of insects a given root
injury is due. The presence of this root worm in the field gives
origin to the usual general effects of the loss of roots by the plant,
varying according to the age of the corn, the gravity of the injury,
and the kind of soil and weather. A conspicuous damage, noticeable on a casual inspection, may vary from the death of the plant
to a slight retardation of its growth or to a general spindling,
yellowish, and unhealthy look.

In the young plant, about six inches high, the characteristic
perforations of the stalk underground may result in the sudden
withering of the whole plant, or, more commonly, in the killing of
the central leaf or tuft of growing leaves—an appearance which
has given to this insect the common name of the " bud worm " in
some of the Southern States. In certain instances the plant has .
been killed, as in Maryland, almost as soon as it has sprouted.

As the season advances, the corn in affected fields is likely to be uneven in size, and later, as the plant becomes top-heavy with growth, it may fall to the earth when the soil is softened by rains, and especially during windy storms. Having once so fallen, it will, if badly injured, fail to rise again; and it may further be seen that the plant has but little hold upon the ground, a whole hill, perhaps, being readily pulled up with one hand. As a consequence of the loss of roots and the general weakening of the plant, many stalks fail to set the ear, or form only a nubbin. The injured plant also matures slowly, remaining green longer than the average, and being thus especially subject to injury by frost.

A closer examination of the young plant will commonly show a perforation of the underground part of the stem either at or near the upper circle of roots. Later, as the corn plant increases in size, the roots themselves are seen to be gnawed irregularly, great holes or notches being eaten out, first in one direction and then in another, until the roots are severed or consumed. In the larger roots the larva may perhaps completely bury itself, but it is much more likely to eat in and out irregularly than is the smaller northern corn root worm presently to be described. It differs from this last species likewise in the fact that it commonly devours everything as it goes, leaving little or no refuse in its burrows; and in the further fact that it works all along to some extent in the base of the stalk, which it penetrates, but not deeply, finally causing the stalk to blacken and rot where water gets admission to its injuries. Its attack on corn is also earlier, briefer, and much more vigorous and destructive, owing to the larger size of the larva and its more rapid growth and earlier maturity. Even in well-grown corn it very commonly bores into the stalk beneath the upper circle of brace roots, or behind the sheath of the lower leaf—habits in which it differs from the northern corn root worm.

Search for this root worm should be made in or about the injured parts—from the middle of May to the middle of August in the latitude of the southern half of Illinois. It is a soft, slender-bodied, worm-like insect, a little over half an inch in length when full grown, and nearly ten times as long as thick. The surface is slightly wrinkled or warty, white when young, and yellowish when old. The head is dark brown, sometimes nearly black, and there is a pale brown leathery patch on the top of the segment next behind the head, and a nearly circular similar patch on the top of the last segment of the body. The legs are very short and small, and the skin bears only a few long scattered hairs.

FIG. 52.—Southern Corn Root Worm, dorsal view; enlarged five diameters.

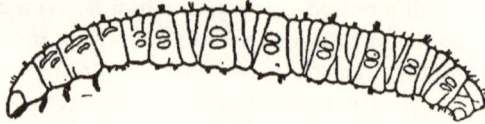

FIG. 53.—The same, side view.

It seems most likely to attack early planted corn, and hence in the Northern States has been found most frequently in sweet corn. An injury of fifty per cent. is a not unusual effect of its presence in Southern Illinois, and elsewhere it has been reported as sometimes destroying almost every hill when the corn was young.

This corn root worm has not been taken in the act of injury to the roots of any other plant than corn, but has once been seen eating off a stem of young wheat in fall.* Lugger found the pupæ among the roots of a common prairie plant, the cone flower (Rudbeckia), but says nothing of injury to that plant; and my assistant, Mr. Marten, reports the occurrence of young larvæ among the roots of *Cyperus strigosus* and *Scirpus fluviatilis*—two sedges common in moist low lands, the roots of which presented the same appearance of injury as those of infested corn.

FIG. 54.—Beetle of Southern Corn Root Worm; enlarged five and two-thirds diameters.

The food of the adult *Diabrotica 12-punctata* is widely varied, apparently much more so than that of the northern Diabrotica. It has been for a long time commonly known as a squash beetle, eating both leaves and green fruit of squashes, melons, and cucumbers. We have seen it eating into pumpkins, sometimes to the depth of half an inch, and feeding upon clover blossoms and upon the leaves of tame and wild sunflowers (Helianthus). We have found it in May eating away the edges of the leaves of young corn in the field, and in July and August making small round holes in corn leaves in our breeding cages. In September and October it has occasionally been taken from the tip of

* Webster, in Bull. 45 (1892), Ohio Agr. Exper. Station, p. 203.

the ear of corn, feeding on the silk, and once in August we saw it gathering up fallen corn pollen. It has also fed upon ragweed leaves in our breeding cages in August. By other observers it has been reported to feed on the petals of various flowers, including roses, dahlias, cosmos, and the cotton plant; upon young volunteer oats (December), on certain moulds, on the horse nettle (*Solanum canadense*), on cabbage, cauliflower, and beans; and on the leaves of plums, cherries, apricots, and raspberries. Webster has also seen it eating unripe kernels of wheat and corn.

LIFE HISTORY.

As is very commonly the case with American injurious insects, the life history of this beetle is incomplete. Our studies of it are deficient not only in continuity of experimental work, but even in a number and distribution of observations and collections, sufficient to give us a fair ground of probable inference. We are especially uncertain as to the number of broods and the stage or stages of hibernation. In the latitudes of Central and Southern Illinois it seems most likely that this is a two-brooded insect, but, if so, data published from Alabama and Mississippi would make it extremely probable that it is three-brooded there. Webster's observations in Indiana would lead us to suppose that it hibernates as an adult, he having found it feeding upon volunteer oats as late as December 14th, and abroad in spring as early as April 17th, at which time the sexes appeared *in copula*.

Our own voluminous collection records of the adult do not clearly bear out the suppositions made above concerning the hibernation and the number of annual generations of this species. Without ever having made any special search for it, I find that we have actually obtained it in eighty-two collections,—mostly of a miscellaneous character,—ranging from April 20th to November 15th. We have thus taken the imago once in April, six times in May, eight times in June, sixteen times in July, twenty-eight in August, eighteen in September, four in October, and once in November—a gradual rise in frequency from April to August, and a similar gradual decline thence to the end of the season. In our special collections of hibernating insects this species has not appeared; and in our large electric-light collections, made from May to September in 1886 and 1887, it occurred infrequently, and in no case until July.

As we now understand the subject we may say that in the latitude of the southern half of the State the eggs are laid in May and June, that the root worms do the greater part of their mischief also in these months, pupating from the middle of June to the last

of July, and yielding the beetle in July and August. The new
generation commence to pair by the beginning of the month last
mentioned, and young larvæ of the generation following may be
found early in September.

I need only add that the eggs are placed, either singly or in
groups of two to twelve or more, according to Riley's observations,
below the surface of the soil near the plants, in cracks or immediately about the base of the plants.

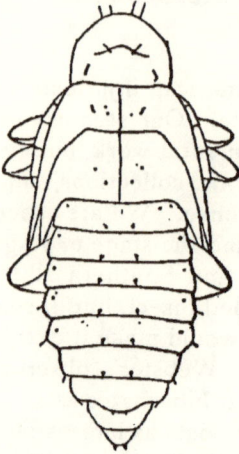

FIG. 55.—Pupa of Southern Corn Root
Worm, dorsal view; enlarged ten
diameters.

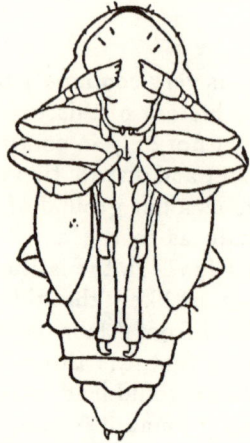

FIG. 56.—Ventral view of same

NATURAL ENEMIES.

So far as now known, the most effective natural check on the
multiplication of this insect is a bacterial parasite (*Bacillus rufans*)
observed by me to infest the larva, killing about three-fourths of
a considerable collection of these corn root worms brought from
Jacksonville July 19, 1889. We do not yet know what part of
the larva is first attacked by this Bacillus, but by the time the
resulting disease has reached a fatal stage, it swarms in all the
fluids of the root worm, which have become practically a pure
culture of this bacterial species. Infested larvæ lose their characteristic yellowish tinge, becoming gray and somewhat swollen, and
after death they change color through pinkish to dull dark red,
the internal organs breaking up to a fluid pulp, held for a considerable time in the tough cuticle of the dead larva. The fluids
of such specimens have a milky appearance in the pale worms and
a reddish tint in the others. This last color is due, not to the
color of the bacilli themselves, but to an excreted coloring matter
diffused through the fluids in which they grow. In artificial

cultures, consequently,—a number of which I made in 1889,—a similar color is imparted to the culture medium, whether this be solid or fluid.

I have discovered no insect enemy of this species, but Dr. Riley reports the rearing of two dipterous parasites of it; one from the larva and pupa, and one (a tachinid) from the beetle. Professor H. Garman notes the occurrence of small numbers of predaceous beetles and larvæ in summer and fall with young root worms in the earth. He also mentions some internal parasites of the imago—Gregarinæ and nematoid worms.

Notwithstanding the abundance of the adult Diabrotica and its general distribution upon a great variety of plants, it seems but little noticed by birds. It has occurred but once in my own studies of the food of· birds (in July, eaten by a catbird), and was not once recognized by Dr. Riley's assistants in their studies of the contents of the stomachs of one hundred and two English sparrows which had eaten insects.

REMEDIAL MEASURES.

Until the life history of this species is better known, measures of prevention or of remedy can scarcely be intelligently discussed. The fact that its injuries to corn occur without apparent reference to the crop of the previous year makes it unlikely that the favorite method of rotation will serve for the protection of corn against this species. According to the scattered observations hitherto reported sweet corn seems to be much more liable to injury than the field varieties, from which fact we may surmise that the time of planting has something to do with the intensity of the attack. The vicinity of cucumbers, squashes, and other of the commoner food plants of the beetle may, however, account for this seeming preference.

c. *Roots visibly penetrated and perforated scarcely at all; sometimes decayed at tips, but not eaten away. Principal injury interior, in form of minute burrows which are commonly longitudinal.*

THE NORTHERN CORN ROOT WORM.
(*Diabrotica longicornis*, Say.)
(FIG. 57–61.)

The northern or common corn root worm (*Diabrotica longicornis*) is by far the most destructive corn root insect dependent on that plant alone. Indeed, it now seems likely that if it were not for the fact that it is highly susceptible to a measure of prevention which farmers have very generally taken unconsciously, as a part of a sound agricultural routine, it would long ago have seriously threatened the profitable continuance of corn culture in the very part of the country best adapted to that great crop. Even as it is, its injuries are undoubtedly to be reckoned by millions of dollars annually*, although the essential facts concerning its ravages and their ready and complete prevention were officially and widely published nine years ago.†

FIG. 57.—Northern Corn Root Worm; enlarged six diameters.

INJURIES TO CORN.

The presence of this insect first betrays itself in badly infested fields when the plant is a foot or so high. If at this time patches of corn are observed which seem to be standing still, so that the plants adjacent leave them behind, giving the field an uneven appearance, it is possible—especially if the field has been in corn two years or more preceding—that this retardation of growth is due to the presence of this corn root worm. In this case, if the corn be pulled up, many of the larger roots will be seen to be short and stubbed and rotten at the ends. On others a deadened brown line will be found, running irregularly lengthwise, while still other roots may be dead their whole length. Possibly when the earth is shaken off a slender white grub will be discovered, two-fifths of an inch long and about as thick as a pin; but more frequently the observer must carefully split or peel some of the affected roots, when a slender sinuous brown burrow filled with excrement will be exposed, running from one end of the root to the other, usually with the root worm just mentioned somewhere in its course. This grub is white, except the head, the top of the first segment of the body, and a little patch on the last segment, which are yellowish brown. The body is smooth and cylindrical, the head is short, deep, and rounded, and the tip of the body is also bluntly rounded off, somewhat like that of a common grub. These last characters will serve to distinguish it from small wireworms which are often found in such situations, but which are usually flattened from above, especially at the head, while in them the end of the body is commonly more or less toothed or notched or pointed. The grubs or larvæ of several

*Webster estimates the damage to corn in twenty-four counties of Indiana in 1885 at $2,000,000, basing this judgment on a loss of $16,000 by one large farmer, and on his personal knowledge of its distribution and abundance in that State.

†Twelfth Rep. State Ent. Ill., pp. 29, 30.

small flies will often be found about the roots of corn, and careless or unskilled observers have occasionally mistaken these for the corn root worm, but this latter insect has six short legs on the three segments just behind the head, while the grubs of flies are footless. We have seen as many as fifteen or twenty to a hill, and I do not doubt that in fields heavily attacked they are much more numerous. As the root dies, however, it is forsaken and another is attacked, until, not infrequently, almost every root will become infested as fast as it puts forth. This damage may thus extend to the practical destruction of the entire root growth, and the consequent death of the plant; or it may remain miserably dwarfed— six inches, perhaps, when other plants measure four or five feet. If the stem is perforated above the roots, the injury is probably due to the southern root worm or to some of the species of wireworms, which one can only be told by finding the insect itself.

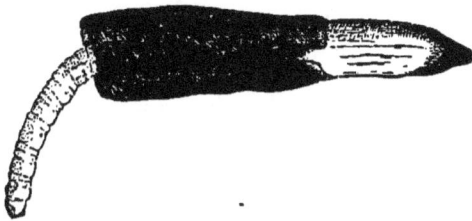

FIG. 58.—Corn root broken across to show Northern Corn Root Worm within.

FIG. 59.—Pupa of Northern Corn Root Worm; enlarged 8½ diameters.

Attention may perhaps be first attracted when the corn is putting forth the silk, by the extraordinary number of barren stalks upon which no ear is forming, or stalks may be seen which have scarcely life enough to tassel. It may also be observed that the corn is unaccountably late, looking evidently greener and younger than other fields which had no advantage at the start. Or injury may be first suspected during a period of drouth, patches here and there, or the entire field, suffering unduly from this cause. The most conspicuous evidence of this injury, however, at this stage of growth, is the prostration of the corn after a soaking rain with wind, and the evident inability of the plant to right itself. If one of the worst affected stalks be pulled up, the observer will notice that the roots are few in number, that many of them are withered and brown, and that others are rotted away to stubs. In these discolored roots the minute brown burrow of the insect may usually be detected, and the corn root worm itself may often be exposed. A minor attack frequently has the effect so to retard the ripening of the corn that it is not ready for the earliest frosts, and the ear consequently remains soft and unfit for use; or the loss of roots may have diminished the size of the stalk and ear, leaving a small nubbin where a full ear might have been expected.

The injury continues from about the first or the middle of June to the last of August. As some of the larvæ mature and cease their work in the latter half of June, and others not for two months later, plants once infested may be freed of the attack, at least in part, by the pupation of the root worms, and others, spared at the beginning of the season, may become infested later. It has sometimes been observed that large, rank stalks which did not ear out had evidently been injured after the corn had begun to tassel; while others, which leaned over at the root and then grew erect, had been infested earlier in the season, but had thrown out new roots after the root worms had matured.

It is a matter of common observation that injuries by this insect are most noticeable during dry years and upon the higher parts of the field. We have no evidence, however, that the corn root worms themselves are more numerous at such times or in such situations, and the greater injury may be due simply to the diminished ability of the plant to withstand attack. I have, in fact, seen vigorous and flourishing hills of corn badly infested during wet seasons with no visible effect upon their growth, even the larger, burrowed roots remaining fresh and efficient, notwithstanding the injury.

In case no retardation of growth or damage to the crop has been observed, less conspicuous mischief may often be indicated by the great abundance in the field, late in July and in August, of a small grass-green beetle about a fifth of an inch in length, resembling in shape and general aspect the common small striped squash beetle, to which, indeed, it is closely allied. These beetles are most likely to be seen clustered at the tip of the ear and feeding upon the young silk, or lurking at the base of the leaf where it joins the stalk, feeding there upon the fallen pollen of the plant. They should also be looked for upon the blossoms of ragweed, smartweed, and other plants in bloom among the corn. This is the adult insect to which the corn root worm, so-called, has given origin, and its presence in extraordinary numbers in any field of corn is presumptive evidence that the plant has suffered earlier considerable root injury of the character above described.

It is very rarely that these phenomena are to be observed on ground not previously in corn, although sorghum and broom corn have been found somewhat favorable to the development of this insect. It is only where through neglect it has become enormously abundant in a f ≥ld that we may anticipate its escape from the corn in very large nⴜmbers before it has laid its eggs, in which event, corn not succeeding corn may possibly suffer the following year.* The general damage to a field is in the worst cases sufficient to destroy the crop so far that the disgusted farmer turns his pigs into his corn to get what they can, and makes no attempt to harvest his crop. A badly infested field was described to me by Dr. Boardman in 1882, which is worthy of mention as illustrating one of the common effects of root injury by this beetle. "I should say," he writes, "that one-fourth of the corn in this field was rotting or beginning to rot. I found, on cutting an ear open, that I could slice the cob as easily as if it were a turnip. The infested corn [in Stark county] is yielding from ten to fifteen bushels per acre."

Although the corn root worm beetle is distributed throughout the Mississippi Valley, and south even to Central America, it clearly becomes comparatively rare southward, and has never been taken by us in Southern Illinois in any numbers, nor found injurious in the larval stage except in the northern two-thirds of the State.

This root worm has not heretofore been certainly found infesting any other plant than corn, and the amount of skilled attention which has been given to this point by entomologists and other accurate observers, makes it practically sure that it is so closely limited to corn at the present time in Illinois that we may base our economic methods upon the supposition that it infests no other plant.

FOOD OF THE BEETLE.

The beetles, beginning to appear in June and continuing until November, feed entirely during this whole period upon the softer and more delicate parts of the vegetation present at the time. They collect the pollen from the tassels of the corn, or gather that which has sifted down among the leaves and collected at their bases, where these join the stalk. They also gnaw away the fresh silk from the tip of the ear (where they may often be found congregated in numbers of a dozen to twenty, or more), probably thus doing a considerable amount of mischief by destroying the silk before it has served for the fertilization of the grain, and causing thus a partial blasting of the ear. They often eat the pollen of smartweed and ragweed among the corn, and outside the

---

* As an example of this tendency to spread from the infested field, I may note the not uncommon occurrence at Rankin, Ill., July 1, 1887, of this corn root worm in a field of corn following oats, but only on that part of it which bordered an infested field in corn the previous year. It is possible that other instances of this kind reported previous to 1891 may have related to the southern corn root worm, *Diabrotica 12-punctata.*

fields are very abundant upon thistle blossoms, and likewise upon heads of red clover, the pollen and petals of which they feed upon. By Professor French, of Carbondale, Ill., they are said sometimes to infest the bean plant; Dr. Boardman, of Stark county, reported them as abundant on cucumber and squash vines; and we have repeatedly seen them late in the year (October 11th to December 16th) gnawing into ripe pumpkins in the field, eating through the outer hard coat, and burying themselves in the pulp to a depth of nearly half an inch. We have found them feeding on flowers of Helianthus, goldenrod, and other Compositæ, and on the pollen of sorghum and of squash; and Professor Webster has seen them on the blossoms of the cotton plant. A farmer in DeKalb county asserts that they eat the pulp of apples where the skin has been broken from some other cause, enlarging such injuries so as seriously to damage the fruit. This same fact was reported to me some years ago from Grundy county, by Mr. O. B. Galusha, then Secretary of the State Horticultural Society, thin-skinned apples apparently suffering worst and, according to the judgment of my informant, being thus injured without the assistance of other insects. They have been repeatedly detected by us beneath the husks of ears of corn, where the tips had been exposed or injured by birds or grasshoppers, feeding here on the broken grains. In one instance the beetle had apparently made its way through the husk itself, and was feeding upon the soft grains beneath. By Professor Burrill, of the University of Illinois, it was found in 1889 (September 30th) feeding upon a fungus belonging to the genus

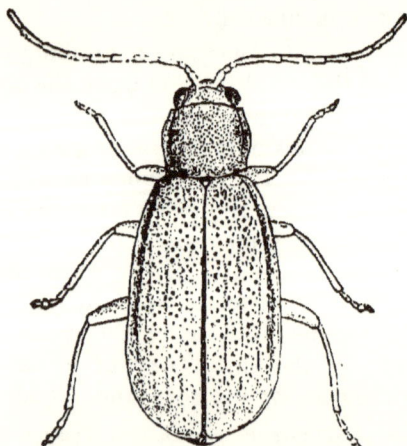

Fig. 60.—Beetle of Northern Corn Root Worm; enlarged ten diameters.

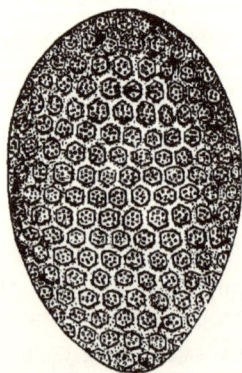

Fig. 61.—Egg of this species; enlarged eighty diameters.

Phallus; and I demonstrated by dissections in 1882 the fact that it sometimes feeds largely on the smaller fungi—blights, rusts, etc.*

LIFE HISTORY.

This species is single-brooded, as far as known. Although a few beetles may occasionally linger late in open winters,—to December 16th of the present year (1892) for example,—and as a rare exception may even pass the winter alive, the species hibernates almost invariably as an egg in the earth.† As a rule, which is, so far as known, practically without exception, these eggs are deposited in fields of corn and hatch there the following spring— at just what date has not been precisely ascertained. The larvæ have first been detected in Central Illinois June 10th. They were found by me less than half grown near Polo, in Northern Illinois, June 14, 1883. As the beetle was reported by an excellent observer (Dr. E. R. Boardman) to have occurred one season in southeastern Iowa as early as June 25th, some larvæ must hatch by the beginning of that month. Pupation can scarcely begin later than June 20th if Dr. Boardman's date for the beetle is correct, and the same observer reports the finding of the pupa itself in the earth June 29th. On the other hand, larvæ ready for pupation have occurred in our collections as late as August 26th—giving a period of something over two months for the pupation of an entire generation.

The extreme dates definitely fixed for the next transformation—the emergence of the beetle—are June 25th for the earliest and not earlier than August 31st for the last—again a period of something more than two months. We have seen the beetles copulating at various dates from July 19th to September 25th,—an interval of two months and six days,—observations which probably fix approximately the beginning and the end of oviposition. The eggs, however, were not all laid by October 1, 1882, as I determined by dissecting females at the time. For the present we may assign August 1st and October 5th as the average dates for the first and last deposit of eggs.

The recognition of this eight or nine weeks' period for the passage of the whole of a brood from one stage to another, enables us to say with some assurance that the eggs laid during this long interval in one year will hatch through a corresponding interval

---

*Twelfth Rep. State Ent. Ill., p. 23.

†I have in my office collection two specimens (one male and one female) obtained March 14, 1883, at Normal, Ill., with a quantity of miscellaneous insects collected from their hibernating quarters. On the other hand, beetles collected from pumpkins at Urbana, November 2, 1892, and placed in breeding cages with pieces of pumpkin as food, had died in large numbers by November 20th; a very few were still alive December 4th; two remained December 17th; but December 28th all were dead.

the year following—approximately from May 15th to July 15th, or a little later. While these dates are, some of them, inferred, there is no doubt of the extension of each stage of the development over as long a period as that here given; namely, two months to nine weeks. We have no precise observations concerning the length of life of any individual in any one stage; neither do we know the number of eggs laid by each female, except as an inference from dissections. I have counted as many as fifty well-formed eggs of nearly full size in the ovaries of a single female beetle.

HABITS OF BEETLE AND LARVA.

The growing larvæ remain concealed from view within the roots, burrowing, not through the middle but nearer the surface, in a slightly sinuous longitudinal direction, sometimes from the stalk outwards, but more frequently mining inwards from the outer end of the root. They have considerable power of locomotion when removed from their burrows, and seem capable of going from one root to another. Indeed, the fact that they must concentrate in hills of corn after hatching, demonstrates their power of locomotion when still very young. It is altogether likely, consequently, that if a hill of corn is killed by them before they have reached maturity, they will be entirely able to search out another.

When full grown they leave the root preliminary to pupation, shortening up and changing to the pupa stage in the dirt close by. At this time they may often be found in considerable numbers by pulling up infested corn and shaking out the dirt from the roots. The beetles emerge from the pupa under ground, and, coming to the surface, most commonly crawl up the stalk of corn adjacent. When recently transformed they are of a pale yellowish color, with scarcely a tinge of green. Their first food consists, as already mentioned, of the softer tissues of the corn plant itself, especially of the silk at the tip of the ear, or the pollen from the tassel, or sometimes of the soft kernels, especially if these have been exposed by any injury to the husks. They also spread to various blossoming weeds in the field, and after a time begin to desert the corn field, scattering elsewhere for food. It is commonly towards the last of August that they are first noticeably frequent on thistle blossoms, heads of clover, and other outside blooming plants. They do not, however, leave the corn fields generally for some time thereafter, but may be found there in greatly diminished numbers at least as late as the middle of October.

How soon after pairing their eggs are laid we do not now know; neither has the process of oviposition ever been directly witnessed. The frequent occurrence of dead female beetles (in October and November) in the earth in corn fields in the midst of the eggs, and the distribution of the eggs themselves, is, however, sufficient evidence that the beetle enters the earth to lay her eggs, and that she may perish there after her ovaries are spent. Although the eggs of this beetle have never been found outside of corn fields, notwithstanding extensive search in many other situations, it is certain that the eggs are not necessarily all laid before the female leaves the field in which she emerged. I have, on the contrary, frequently proven by dissection of beetles taken from flowers by roadsides, in meadows, and the like, that females thus dispersed may still contain eggs in large numbers. A considerable part of the beetles, and apparently the greater part, do, however, lay their eggs under ordinary circumstances before they leave the field of corn; and it is also highly probable on general grounds that those which go elsewhere in search of food return to corn fields for oviposition. Since the larva is not known to infest any other plant than corn, or, indeed, to be capable of living upon any other, it is altogether likely that the female instinctively searches out the corn plant when seeking a place of deposit for her eggs.

As this is a surmise or inference, however, and not a matter of observation, it remains possible that if the corn root worm is neglected it may in time accumulate in such numbers as no longer to confine its chief injuries to fields previously in corn, but that the beetles, forced to scatter early, in search of food, from the fields in which they emerge will deposit their eggs freely everywhere in the ground, instead of being confined as now chiefly to corn fields. It is probably in fields of clover that this is most likely to occur, since the beetles sometimes become abundant there, feeding upon the pollen of the second growth.

The depth at which the eggs are laid varies from an inch to five or six inches, the greater part of them being near the surface of the ground. They are usually deposited in bunches of three or four to eight or ten, within a space of half an inch across, not in contact with each other, nor in any cell or cavity, but always simply scattered in the earth. Most careful examinations made in 1882, and many times repeated, of the earth between the rows, and of the roots of all the weeds growing in the field, have failed to discover so much as a single egg outside a space a few inches across, around each hill. A similar careful search of the roots of thistles, ragweeds, and goldenrod outside the fields, upon the flowers of which the beetles were feeding in great numbers, had a similar result; and we have found no evidence in the roots of these plants, either in the corn fields or elsewhere, that they have ever been infested by the larvæ. In short, not the slightest direct proof has thus far been found that the beetle breeds anywhere except in fields of corn. It is very probable that a few develop in other situations; but the number seems to be so small as to defy discovery, except by accident.

PREVENTION AND REMEDY.

A judicious rotation of crops is so simple and complete a preventive measure, that *remedies* for injury to corn by the northern corn root worm are practically unnecessary. The eggs being laid in corn ground in the fall and the larvæ hatching the following spring, feeding so far as known upon nothing else but corn, the planting of such infested land to any other grain must inevitably lead to the starvation of the young when they hatch in spring. This is not an inference from the life history of the insect merely, but even before the time and place of oviposition were known, it had been commonly noticed that corn was rarely if ever liable to injury by this insect if planted on ground which had borne any other kind of crop the preceding year. I have, however, some reason to suppose that sorghum and broom corn are not good crops to follow with corn when this root worm is present.

The frequency of the rotation must depend upon circumstances, and especially upon the general abundance of the insect at the time. I know of no part of Illinois in which corn is not safe for at least two years, and in many situations another year may be added to this period. No field on which the crop has already suffered to any noticeable extent should be planted to corn the following year; and it will likewise be prudent to avoid continuing in corn any field in which the grass-green beetle of this species is seen to be abundant in September and October.

The only other preventive measure worthy of mention is one equally to be commended as a general agricultural practice; namely, the maintenance of the fertility of the soil by the use of manures, etc. This will not, so far as known, diminish in any way the amount of insect attack, but it will enable the plant to stand a minor injury with relatively little loss. It is possible that experiments with various kinds of fertilizers will show that some of them, the potash salts for instance, may have an immediate deleterious effect upon the larvæ in the earth, but we have at present only a speculative basis for this supposition.

S. A. FORBES, PH. D.,
Consulting Entomologist.